New Mexico Bucket List Adventure Guide

Explore 100 Offbeat Destinations You Must Visit!

Tyler Herrera

Canyon Press
canyon@purplelink.org

Please consider writing a review!
Just visit: purplelink.org/review

ISBN: 978-1-957590-13-4

FREE BONUS

Discover 31 Incredible Places You Can
Visit Next! Just Go To:

purplelink.org/travel

Table of Contents:

How to Use This Book

Welcome to your very own adventure guide to exploring the many wonders of the state of New Mexico. Not only does this book offer the most wonderful places to visit and sights to see in the vast state, but it provides GPS coordinates for Google Maps to make exploring that much easier.

Adventure Guide
Sorted by region, this guide offers over 100 amazing wonders found in New Mexico for you to see and explore. They can be visited in any order, and this book will help you keep track of where you've been and where to look forward to going next. Each section describes the area or place, what to look for, how to get there, and what you may need to bring along.

GPS Coordinates
As you can imagine, not all of the locations in this book have a physical address. Fortunately, some of our listed wonders are either located within a National Park or Reserve or near a city, town, or place of business. For those that are not associated with a specific location, it is easiest to map it using GPS coordinates.

Luckily, Google has a system of codes that converts the coordinates into pin-drop locations that Google Maps can interpret and navigate.

Each adventure in this guide includes GPS coordinates along with a physical address whenever it is available.

It is important that you are prepared for poor cell signals. It is recommended that you route your location and ensure that the directions are accessible offline. Depending on your device and the distance of some locations, you may need to travel with a backup battery source.

About New Mexico

Originally colonized by Spain, New Mexico became a United States territory in 1853 as part of the Gadsden Purchase. Even though the land was considered part of the U.S., it officially became the 47th state in 1912. Home to over 2 million people, New Mexico, sits in the southwestern reaches of the country. Because of its lush landscape and culture, New Mexico has been nicknamed the "Land of Enrichment." In addition to its beautiful landscape, rich culture, and endless attractions, New Mexico also has a unique history.

During World War II, the Manhattan Project began its nuclear research on New Mexico's soil, where scientists raced to create the world's most powerful—and devastating—bomb. On July 16, 1945, the first atomic bomb was tested at the Trinity bomb site near the city of Alamagordo. It is said that people who lived over 150 miles from the test site could feel the impact of the explosion.

New Mexico has also, reportedly, had mysterious encounters with possible extraterrestrial life. In 1947, a local farmer from Roswell found unusual debris on his property and claimed it was the remains of an alien spaceship. While the U.S. Air Force claimed it was simply a crashed air balloon, others knew that it was virtually impossible for a human to survive that height of a crash and even used test-dummy experiments to prove it. Since then, the town of Roswell has become a popular destination for those interested in extraterrestrial life.

Because of its endless options for tourism and activities, New Mexico is a prime destination for road trippers, families, and adventurers alike. Outdoor enthusiasts can explore New Mexico's numerous national forests and parks, ski at its eight resorts, go white-water rafting, and camp in the backcountry wilderness. At night, the stars fill the sky in a way that cannot be found in major cities. For the ultimate sky-gazing experience, visit one of New Mexico's Dark Sky Parks.

For those interested in the state's unique history, New Mexico has several Native American museums that promote the art, pueblos, and culture of these sovereign nations. New Mexico is well known for its art communities, and enthusiasts can explore its many art museums and attractions. Not only can visitors interact with artists who are inspired by New Mexico's culture, but they can also visit the home of Georgia O'Keeffe, who was enamored with New Mexico and moved to the state's capital of Santa Fe to be closer to the landscape.

For tourists who are interested in a spooky historical experience, a visit to one of New Mexico's 400 ghost towns is a must. Most of these towns sprang up during the rush to mine gold, silver, copper, lead, coal, and turquoise. Many were suddenly abandoned, and their populations vanished. To see bits of history, remnants of towns, and old mining equipment, visitors should explore New Mexico's ghost towns.

Landscape and Climate

New Mexico spans 121,590 square miles and is the fifth-largest state in the United States. It is composed of six separate regions: Northwest, North Central, Northeast, Central, Southwest, and Southeast. New Mexico is situated in the southernmost part of the United States and shares borders with Arizona to the west and Texas to the east. Additionally, this state shares a border with Mexico.

New Mexico offers a diverse landscape that includes heavily forested mountains and vast, arid deserts. With three distinct topographical regions, New Mexico has varied environments that any visitor can appreciate. The Rocky Mountain zone spans across the north-central part of New Mexico and offers gorgeous mountain views. It may be one of New Mexico's most stunning features. There are 23 mountain ranges in total, such as San Juan and Sacramento.

The plains region covers most of New Mexico and extends from the eastern border to the Sangre de Cristos and the Guadalupe mountain ranges. The Great Plains cover about one-third of New Mexico's landscape and are characterized by large flatlands with few trees and little change in elevation.

In addition to the plains and mountains, the third topographical region of New Mexico is the intermountain plateau, which is an elevated area that is generally found between mountains.

The elevation ranges from 2,817 feet at Red Bluff Lake to New Mexico's highest peak, Wheeler Peak, at 13,161 feet. Elephant Butte Lake is New Mexico's largest lake at nearly

40 miles long, and it includes more than 200 miles of shoreline.

New Mexico's climate is dry and does not experience extreme weather conditions. When it comes to sunshine, it's one of the sunniest states in the country. In fact, New Mexico comes in second place behind Arizona for most days of sunshine each year.

Because of its elevation, New Mexico does have four seasons. Generally, the weather will include hot days that cool off overnight. During the summer, the occasional scattered thunderstorm is to be expected. In the winter, the weather will stay moderate, though some areas will get heavy snow. While spring and fall feature some of the most gorgeous weather (65°F to 85°F), spring is known for being more unpredictable in terms of temperature and precipitation.

While the highest temperature recorded in New Mexico is 122°F, the average temperature in the summer is around 97°F, and it's not uncommon for hot summer days to consistently exceed 100°F. In the winter, the temperature will drop below freezing (less than 0°F) in many places. In fact, the record coldest temperature ever recorded in New Mexico was -50°F. However, the winter temperatures are milder in lower elevations.

Temperatures will vary greatly from day to night because of the effect of the sun and low humidity. Altitude also plays a major role. While higher altitudes have cooler temperatures, lower altitudes feature warmer to more moderate temperatures.

Ghost Ranch

From art tours featuring the work of Georgia O'Keeffe to a wellness retreat to an education center with dinosaurs, Ghost Ranch has it all. Not only does Ghost Ranch offer an on-site campsite, but it has rustic-style lodging accommodations as well. Visitors can go on guided hikes across the landscape, get a massage in the wellness center, visit the Ruth Hall Museum of Paleontology, or even take a sunset trail ride on horseback.

Best Time to Visit: If you visit in the fall, you'll get some of the mildest weather, but many visitors also go during late spring and summer. Because New Mexico stays rather warm year-round, you can go during the winter as well.

Pass/Permit/Fees: Visitors at Ghost Ranch will pay for each activity as well as their accommodations.

Closest City or Town: Abiquiu

Address: 280 Private Drive 1708, Highway US-84, Abiquiu, NM 87510

GPS Coordinates: 36.3137° N, 106.4820° W

Did You Know? Many dinosaur fossils have been found in the dinosaur quarry at Ghost Ranch. In fact, archeologists have uncovered some of the world's largest dinosaur fossil collections here. Ghost Ranch is the location of the only complete *Coelophysis,* which happens to be New Mexico's state fossil.

White Sands National Park

Because of its vast white sand dunes, this park is breathtaking. At the center of the Tularosa Basin, White Sands is the largest gypsum sand dune field. Gypsum sand is rare because it easily dissolves when it comes into contact with water, making this spot truly unique.

The park itself is situated between several military bases, which sometimes causes it to be closed due to missile tests. So, before making the journey to White Sands, visitors should always check online for park closures.

Best Time to Visit: White Sands National Monument is open every day of the year except December 25th. The weather will be warm year-round, but the ideal time to visit White Sands for mild temperatures is in October/November.

Pass/Permit/Fees: White Sands charges a $25 fee per vehicle upon entering the park, but if there is just one person in the car, the fee is only $15. There are options for annual passes.

Closest City or Town: Alamogordo

Address: Alamogordo Visitors Center, 1376 E Ninth Street, Alamogordo, NM 88310

GPS Coordinates: 32.78796° N, 106.32572° W

Did You Know? In 1933, White Sands was declared a national monument. But in 2019, it was renamed a national park.

ABQ BioPark Botanic Garden

The ABQ BioPark Botanic Garden opened in 1996 as part of the ABQ BioPark Zoo and has grown to 32 acres of exhibits. It highlights plants from the American southwest, but there are also numerous plants from around the world. Visitors can explore 1.5 miles of paths through both formal and whimsical gardens such as the Old World Walled Gardens, the Mediterranean Conservatory, the Desert Conservatory, the Camino de Colores, the Rio Grande Heritage Farm, the Sasebo Japanese Garden, the Curandera Garden, the Railroad Garden, the Children's Fantasy Garden, the Cottonwood Gallery, and more.

Best Time to Visit: The ABQ BioPark Botanic Garden is open daily from 9:00 a.m. to 4:00 p.m.

Pass/Permit/Fees: Adult resident admission is $10 per person, and adult nonresident admission is $14.50 per person. Youth residents between the ages of 3 and 12 are $5 per person, and youth nonresidents are $6 per person.

Closest City or Town: Albuquerque

Address: 2601 Central Avenue NW, Albuquerque, NM 87104

GPS Coordinates: 35.09320° N, 106.68149° W

Did You Know? The BUGarium at the ABQ BioPark Botanic Garden immerses visitors in the lives of arthropods and allows them to see the hidden life of bugs from around the world.

Albuquerque Museum

The Albuquerque Museum opened in 1967 as a concept created by a group of community members who wanted to preserve, share, and continue the history and culture of the area. It was originally housed in the old Albuquerque Municipal Airport but has since moved to its current home in the center of Old Town Albuquerque. The museum's collection boasts 10,000 works of art, 27,000 historical artifacts, and over 130,000 photographs that tell the story of the city and its unprecedented growth. Its permanent exhibits include *Casa San Ysidro: The Gutierrez/Minge House*, *Photo Archives Collection*, *History Collection*, and *Art Collection*.

Best Time to Visit: The Albuquerque Museum is open Tuesday through Sunday from 9:00 a.m. to 5:00 p.m.

Pass/Permit/Fees: Admission is $6 for adults, $4 for seniors ages 65 and older, and $3 for children between the ages of 4 and 12. Children ages three and under are free.

Closest City or Town: Albuquerque

How to get there: 2000 Mountain Road NW, Albuquerque, NM 87104

GPS Coordinates: 35.09823° N, 106.66829° W

Did You Know? The Outdoor Sculpture Garden features large-scale art in metal, stone, and earthen materials by Allan Houser, Glenna Goodacre, Luis Jimenez, and Nora Naranjo Morse. It's open year-round.

Cliff's Amusement Park

Cliff's Amusement Park is Albuquerque's premier location for thrill rides and water slides. It offers more than 50 rides and attractions for everyone from toddlers to senior citizens. Some of the most popular thrill rides include Downdraft, Cliff Hanger, New Mexico Rattler, Musik Express, SideWinder, and Fire Ball. Family-friendly attractions include the Carousel, Demolition Disco, Falling Star, Galaxi, Sea Dragon, and Rocky Mountain Rapids. Kiddyland is an excellent spot for younger children who aren't quite ready for the big rides. They can enjoy Spin-O-Rama, Baja Buggy, The Balloon Wheel, Doggie-Go-Round, The Frog Hopper, Happy Swing, and others. In addition to the water park, there is also the Vault Lazer Maze Challenge, Frog Fishing, Gravity Ball, Whac-A-Mole, and various other midway games.

Best Time to Visit: The hours of operation for Cliff's Amusement Park vary from 11:00 a.m. to 7:00 p.m., depending on the day. Check the website calendar for hours.

Pass/Permit/Fees: The fee to visit Cliff's Amusement Park is between $25 and $30 per person.

Closest City or Town: Albuquerque

Address: 4800 Osuna Road NE, Albuquerque, NM 87109

GPS Coordinates: 35.14404° N, 106.58817° W

Did You Know? Cliff's Amusement Park first opened under the name Uncle Cliff's Amusement Park in 1959. It has the only wooden rollercoaster in the state.

Downtown Growers' Market

For 25 years, the Downtown Growers' Market in Albuquerque has been providing the community with a wide selection of local meats, produce, eggs, and honey. Visitors are also exposed to the best small businesses in New Mexico. Each week, packaged and freshly prepared food and drink are made available to buyers from all walks of life. The market accepts EBT/SNAP, WIC, Senior, and FreshRX benefits and can double your spending with the help of the Double Up Food Bucks Program. Local artists and body-care vendors are also on-site to provide entertainment and health products to attendees.

Best Time to Visit: The Downtown Growers' Market is open every Saturday between mid-April and early November from 8:00 a.m. to 12:00 p.m.

Pass/Permit/Fees: There is no fee to visit the Downtown Growers' Market but be sure to bring money to shop.

Closest City or Town: Albuquerque

Address: 810 Copper Avenue NW, Albuquerque, NM 87102

GPS Coordinates: 35.08645° N, 106.65676° W

Did You Know? The Downtown Growers' Market is the longest-running growers' market in Albuquerque and features more than 70 New Mexican growers and 200 local vendors (including artists and artisans) each week.

Gravity Park

Gravity Park is a state-of-the-art trampoline park that provides hours of entertainment and fitness to visitors of all ages. Whether you're looking for an intense individual workout or a fun, energetic activity for your kids, Gravity Park delivers. At the indoor facility, you'll find an open jump area, a Ninja Obstacle Course, Extreme Dodgeball, Slackline, Trapeze, AirDunk, Aerial Skills, Foam Pits, and more. There is a special hour just for kids under the age of 6 before the facility opens to the rest of the public.

Best Time to Visit: For kids ages six and under, the best time to visit the park is Monday through Saturday between 9:00 a.m. and 10:00 a.m. For all other ages, Gravity Park is open Monday through Saturday from 10:00 a.m. to 9:00 p.m. and Sunday from 11:00 a.m. to 7:00 p.m. On Friday and Saturday nights from 9:00 p.m. to 11:00 p.m., only guests ages 15 and older are allowed in the facility.

Pass/Permit/Fees: The fee to visit Gravity Park ranges from $11 to $22 for kids under the age of 6 and from $14 to $28 for guests ages seven and older.

Closest City or Town: Albuquerque

Address: 5300 Eagle Rock Avenue NE, Albuquerque, NM 87113

GPS Coordinates: 35.13272° N, 106.61610° W

Did You Know? An adult accompanying a child under the age of 6 can jump for free!

Indian Pueblo Cultural Center

The Indian Pueblo Cultural Center is known as the "Gateway to the 19 Pueblos of New Mexico" and is dedicated to preserving Pueblo culture by presenting the accomplishments and history of the Pueblo people. The center sits on about 80 acres of land owned by the 19 Pueblos and consists of a museum, a gallery space, a library, archives, an education department, and a teaching kitchen and restaurant. The museum is home to a collection of murals and Native American art and artifacts. It hosts numerous cultural programs and events throughout the year. The center is located in the middle of Albuquerque's business district and operates several additional commercial enterprises in the area, including Four Winds (a convenience store), the Indian Pueblo Store (an art store), Avanyu Plaza (an outdoor gathering space), and Extra Space Storage (a storage facility), among others.

Best Time to Visit: The Indian Pueblo Cultural Center is open Tuesday through Sunday from 9:00 a.m. to 4:00 p.m.

Pass/Permit/Fees: Adult admission is $10 per person. Students, youth, and seniors are $7 per person, and children under the age of 5 are free.

Closest City or Town: Albuquerque

Address: 2401 12th Street NW, Albuquerque, NM 87104

GPS Coordinates: 35.11063° N, 106.65922° W

Did You Know? The 19 Pueblos of New Mexico are each a separate sovereign nation.

Kasha-Katuwe Tent Rocks National Monument

Kasha-Katuwe Tent Rocks National Monument is an outdoor laboratory that provides opportunities for visitors to learn about how the landscapes were shaped and developed. The two trails at Kasha-Katuwe are for foot traffic only and allow for excellent hiking, birdwatching, and scenic views.

The rock formation in Kasha-Katuwe was formed by volcanic activity that occurred nearly 6 to 7 million years ago. These eruptions left pumice, ash, and tuff deposits that are over 1,000 feet thick in some places. Additionally, the volcanic activity left huge rock fragments scattered around the land.

Best Time to Visit: The summer months are the most popular time to visit Kasha-Katuwe, but the park is open year-round. In the summer, there may be less parking than during other times of the year.

Pass/Permit/Fees: There is a $5 fee for private vehicles to enter the park.

Closest City or Town: Albuquerque

Address: 100 Sun Avenue NE, Albuquerque, NM 87109

GPS Coordinates: 35.6143° N, 106.3583° W

Did You Know? In some places, the tent rocks are up to 90 feet tall and are starting to disintegrate because their tents have lost their weather-resistant caprocks.

New Mexico Museum of Natural History & Science

Located near Old Town Albuquerque, the New Mexico Museum of Natural History & Science was established in 1986 and features a permanent exhibit that takes visitors on a journey through time. Starting with *Universe in Origins*, visitors will travel through a range of exhibits: *Dawn of the Dinosaurs, Jurassic Age of Super Giants, New Mexico's Seacoast, Age of Volcanoes, Rise of the Recent – Evolving Grasslands, Cave Experience*, and *New Mexico's Ice Age*. Additional permanent exhibits include the planetarium, *Fossilworks*, the Naturalist Center, and a geologic display of regional minerals.

Best Time to Visit: The museum is open Wednesday through Sunday from 10:00 a.m. to 4:00 p.m.

Pass/Permit/Fees: Admission is $8 per person for adults, $7 for youth ages 13 to 17, $7 for seniors ages 60 and older, and $5 for children ages 3 to 12. There are additional fees for the theater and planetarium.

Closest City or Town: Albuquerque

Address: 1801 Mountain Road NW, Albuquerque, NM 87104

GPS Coordinates: 35.09902° N, 106.66578° W

Did You Know? The museum is home to several complete dinosaur skeletons, including those of a Seismosaurus, a Stegosaurus, and a Saurophaganax. There is also a complete leg skeleton of a Brachiosaurus.

16

Paseo del Bosque Trail

This multipurpose trail in the heart of Albuquerque offers 16 miles of paved pathways that extend from the north of the metro area to the south, taking users through the Rio Grande's cottonwood bosque forest. The trail also passes through Rio Grande Valley State Park near the Rio Grande Nature Center, the Albuquerque BioPark, and the National Hispanic Cultural Center. Walkers, runners, cyclists, skaters, and equestrians frequent this trail that follows the Rio Grande. There are numerous access points such as Alameda Boulevard, Montano Road, Paseo Del Norte, Central Avenue NE, Campbell Road, and Marquez Street. There are parking areas at each access point, making the trail a great option for partial commutes.

Best Time to Visit: The best time to visit the Paseo del Bosque Trail is during the spring, summer, or fall when the weather is best.

Pass/Permit/Fees: There is no fee to visit the Paseo del Bosque Trail.

Closest City or Town: Albuquerque

Address: Albuquerque Visitor Center, 20 First Plaza NW, Suite 601, Albuquerque, NM 87102

GPS Coordinates: 35.14203° N, 106.67736° W

Did You Know? The Paseo del Bosque Trail features public art along the path, and it's uninterrupted by road crossings, making it one of the safest urban trails in the country.

Petroglyph National Monument

Petroglyph National Monument is the site of one of the largest collections of petroglyphs in North America. The symbols and carvings protected by the park are between 400 and 700 years old and were carved by both Indigenous Americans and Spanish settlers. In the park, visitors can go to Boca Negra Canyon, Rinconada Canyon, or Piedras Marcadas Canyon to see these ancient carvings. Additionally, you can hike around the site of cinder cone volcanoes.

Best Time to Visit: The fall and spring will have the mildest weather; summer temperatures can reach up to 99°F.

Pass/Permit/Fees: There is a $1 parking fee on weekdays and a $2 parking fee on weekends. Otherwise, there are no entrance fees to visit the park.

Closest City or Town: Albuquerque

Address: 6001 Unser Boulevard NW, Albuquerque, NM 87120

GPS Coordinates: 35.1368° N, 106.7405° W

Did You Know? The Volcano Day Use Area is comprised of three separate trails: Volcanoes Trail, JA Volcano, Albuquerque Overlook, and Vulcan Volcano Loop. Dogs are allowed at the Volcano Day Use Area as long as they are on a leash, and their owners pick up after their waste.

Sandia Peak Ski Area & Tramway

For a panoramic view of the Sandia Mountains, Albuquerque, and beyond, take a tram ride to the 10,378-foot Sandia Peak. It takes just 15 minutes to ride from the bottom to the top, but you'll marvel at the scenery. Once you get to the top, you have access to more than 100 hiking trails ranging from easy to difficult to accommodate hikers of all abilities. Even if it's warm in Albuquerque, you'll still want to bring a jacket, if not a winter coat. When you step out of the tram, the temperature can be up to 30 degrees cooler than in the city. Additionally, there are 25 miles of ski slopes and trails at Sandia Peak Ski Area that are accessible only by tramway.

Best Time to Visit: The Sandia Peak Ski Area & Tramway is open Wednesday through Monday from 9:00 a.m. to 8:00 p.m.

Pass/Permit/Fees: The fee for a round-trip tram ride is $29 for adults, $19 for children between the ages of 2 and 12, $24 for children between the ages of 13 and 20, and $24 for seniors ages 62 and older. One-way tickets are $18 for all ages. Children under the age of 2 are free.

Closest City or Town: Albuquerque

Address: 30 Tramway Road, Albuquerque, NM 87122

GPS Coordinates: 35.21174° N, 106.41241° W

Did You Know? TEN 3, the restaurant at the top of Sandia Peak, provides drinks, appetizers, and dining options in one of the most scenic eateries in the U.S. at nearly 10,500 feet in altitude.

San Felipe de Neri Church

The San Felipe de Neri Church was built in 1793 and is considered the "crown jewel" of New Mexico. The San Felipe de Neri parish has been serving the Albuquerque community since 1706, following the settlement of 30 families in 1704 and 1705. The church was originally named Francisco Xavier by Don Francisco Cuervo y Valdez, the founder of Albuquerque, but the Duke of Albuquerque ordered the name be changed to San Felipe de Neri to honor the King of Spain. The original building collapsed in 1792 when the area experienced an extremely rainy summer. The new church, which still stands today, was constructed in the shape of a cross and made out of adobe with 5-foot-thick walls. Throughout the years, several buildings have been added to the original structure, including a 2-story convent, a portico, a second-story rectory, a 30-foot porch, and more.

Best Time to Visit: The San Felipe de Neri Church is open for visitation and prayer daily from 10:00 a.m. to 4:00 p.m.

Pass/Permit/Fees: There is no fee to visit the San Felipe de Neri Church.

Closest City or Town: Albuquerque

Address: 2005 N Plaza Street NW, Albuquerque, NM 87104

GPS Coordinates: 35.09714° N, 106.66965° W

Did You Know? Following the Civil War, the Union army leased the San Felipe de Neri Church rectory as a base of western operations for several years.

The American International Rattlesnake Museum

The American International Rattlesnake Museum is an animal-conservation facility that celebrates the myriad ways that rattlesnakes have influenced the world around us. Examples of how snakes have been a positive force throughout history are presented through memorabilia, artifacts, and "the largest collection of different species of live rattlesnakes in the world." The museum has taken care to re-create the natural habitats of rattlesnakes.

Best Time to Visit: Between September and May, the museum is open Monday through Friday from 11:30 a.m. to 5:30 p.m., Saturday from 10:00 a.m. to 6:00 p.m., and Sunday from 1:00 p.m. to 5:00 p.m. In the summer, it's open Monday through Saturday from 10:00 a.m. to 6:00 p.m. and Sunday from 1:00 p.m. to 5:00 p.m.

Pass/Permit/Fees: Admission is $6 per person for adults, $4 for children, and $5 for seniors, military members, students, and teachers.

Closest City or Town: Albuquerque

Address: 202 San Felipe NW, Suite A, Albuquerque, NM 87104

GPS Coordinates: 35.09630° N, 106.66965° W

Did You Know? The American International Rattlesnake Museum has more varieties of rattlesnake than the National Zoo, and those in the Bronx, Philadelphia, San Francisco, San Diego, and Denver combined!

The Explora Science Museum and Children's Museum

With more than 250 interactive STEM exhibits, there's something fun for everyone at the Explora Science Museum and Children's Museum. This experiential learning center is located in Old Town Albuquerque and offers exhibits like *Mechanics Alive, Water Flow Patio, Engineering Gravity, Water of Life, Life of Water, Math Moves, Charges, Currents, and Circuits, Light, Shadow, Color,* and more. Additionally, Explora hosts or facilitates over 2,200 programs for 70,000 guests from all over New Mexico each year. These programs can take place at Explora, at community sites, or online. The museum also provides these programs in both English and Spanish to expand its community reach.

Best Time to Visit: The museum is open Tuesday through Sunday from 10:00 a.m. to 5:00 p.m.

Pass/Permit/Fees: Admission is $7 for adults and $6 for children between the ages of 1 and 11. Children under the age of 1 are free.

Closest City or Town: Albuquerque

Address: 1701 Mountain Road NW, Albuquerque, NM 87104

GPS Coordinates: 35.09851° N, 106.66421° W

Did You Know? Explora was named Best Recreational Program for Kids by *The Alibi*, an Albuquerque-based newspaper.

The National Museum of Nuclear Science & History

As a Smithsonian Affiliate, the National Museum of Nuclear Science & History is the only congressionally chartered museum in the field of nuclear science in the nation. It's the national repository for nuclear science information and is dedicated to presenting exhibits and educational programs on topics related to nuclear science. Originally, the museum was housed at an abandoned repair facility for anti-aircraft guns and was called the Sandia Atomic Museum. It moved to the Albuquerque museum district in 2001, but it did not have enough space for its exhibits. In 2009, a larger museum building was opened.

Best Time to Visit: The museum is open daily from 9:00 a.m. to 5:00 p.m.

Pass/Permit/Fees: Admission is $15 for adults, $11 for children between the ages of 6 and 17, and $13 for seniors ages 60 and older. Children ages five and under are free. Reduced-price admission is available at $7 for military personnel and $8 for veterans.

Closest City or Town: Albuquerque

Address: 601 Eubank Boulevard SE, Albuquerque, NM 87123

GPS Coordinates: 35.06662° N, 106.53363° W

Did You Know? Permanent exhibits include *Cold War*, *Pioneers of the Atom*, *The Decision to Drop*, *Nuclear Medicine*, and more.

Turquoise Museum

The Turquoise Museum has the largest collection of top-grade American turquoise in the world, most of which comes from J.C. "Zack" Zachary Jr. and his father's private collections. Zack learned how to cut turquoise from his father when he was nine years old, and in 1948, he opened his first cutting shop in his garage. Jesse Zachary Sr. managed the Ville Grove Turquoise Mine in Colorado, but when he moved back to New Mexico, he traded in turquoise, Native American arts and crafts, and jewelry. The art passed to the third generation when Zack's son Bob created Zachary Turquoise, Inc. Bob's artwork is on display at the Turquoise Museum.

Best Time to Visit: The museum is open for self-guided tours on Monday, Tuesday, Wednesday, Friday, and Saturday at 11:00 a.m., 12:00 p.m., 1:00 p.m., and 2:00 p.m. Tickets must be pre-purchased online.

Pass/Permit/Fees: Admission is $20 per person or $15 for children up to age 17 and seniors ages 55 and older.

Closest City or Town: Albuquerque

Address: 400 2nd Street SW, Albuquerque, NM 87102

GPS Coordinates: 35.08085° N, 106.64978° W

Did You Know? Joe Lowry, Katy Lowry, and Joe Dan Lowry, nieces and nephews from the second generation of Zacharys, founded the museum and have curated the displays ever since.

24

Veterans' Memorial Park

Considered a hidden gem of Albuquerque, Veterans' Memorial Park is located in the middle of a business district and offers a quiet spot for reflection. It is one of the most underrated outdoor spaces in the city and includes a museum, conference center, and amphitheater. The 25-acre park features numerous public art installations that honor those who have served in the U.S. military. The park was designed to commemorate and showcase veterans' shared experiences, such as those centered on the decision to join the military and their return home. There is an intended route to follow, although choosing to explore the park at your own pace and order does not diminish the experience.

Best Time to Visit: The best time to visit Veterans' Memorial Park is when the Visitors' Center and Museum are open, which is on Friday, Saturday, Sunday, and Monday from 9:00 a.m. to 3:00 p.m.

Pass/Permit/Fees: There is no fee to visit Veterans' Memorial Park or the museum.

Closest City or Town: Albuquerque

Address: 1100 Louisiana SE, Albuquerque, NM 87108

GPS Coordinates: 35.06581° N, 106.56667° W

Did You Know? There are 17 monuments in Veterans' Memorial Park that pay respect to past, present, and future veterans. Specifically, there are monuments to the Navajo Code Talkers, Buffalo Soldiers, and Paratroopers, among 14 others.

Wildlife West Nature Park

Wildlife West Nature Park is a 122-acre wildlife refuge near Albuquerque. Because it's a wildlife refuge and rescue, this attraction features over 20 animals that are native to New Mexico. For example, visitors may see cougars, wolves, bears, elk, deer, javelina, fox, raptors, and much more. The park does offer overnight excursions, but these are only available by appointment.

Best Time to Visit: The park is open from 10 a.m. to 6 p.m. from March 15th through the end of October. It has limited hours from November through mid-March.

Pass/Permit/Fees: Admission to the park costs $9 for adults, $7 for seniors, and $5 for students. Children under age 5 are free.

Closest City or Town: Albuquerque

Address: 87 N. Frontage Road, Edgewood, NM 87015

GPS Coordinates: 35.0696° N, 106.2054° W

Did You Know? If you're interested, you can rent out the entire park for large events, such as weddings, family reunions, corporate events, and more. When you rent it out, you'll get the entire park to yourself, plus wagon rides, private animal shows, and several activities for young children.

Chaco Canyon

Chaco Canyon is the site of numerous historical ruins. In fact, there are ten major sites that visitors can learn about and explore. To see the ruins, visitors can take an 8-mile loop trail that goes right next to these ancient villages. Additionally, the park features four separate trails that explore the entire area. These trails include the Wijiji, South Mesa, Pueblo Alto, and Peñasco Blanco. While the Peñasco Blanco Trail is the one that will take you to the ancient ruins, all the trails feature the gorgeous mesa landscape and Chacoan roads.

Best Time to Visit: You can visit the park year-round, but it will be the most crowded in the summer months.

Pass/Permit/Fees: The park charges $25 for a 7-day vehicle pass.

Closest City or Town: Bloomfield

Address: 1808 CR 7950, Nageezi, NM 87037

GPS Coordinates: 36.0530° N, 107.9559° W

Did You Know? The ruins of Chaco are some of the best-preserved sites of ancient architecture. They were built along the wall of a canyon in the high desert. These ruins feature some very advanced architecture and technology; some are up to 5 stories high and have hundreds of rooms that people once inhabited.

Caballo Lake State Park

For camping, hiking, kayaking, boating, canoeing, swimming, and fishing, Caballo Lake State Park is a fantastic place to visit. Located 20 miles downstream from Elephant Butte and featuring the Caballo Mountains as its background, this lake has some incredible scenic views. Not only is the area known for birdwatching, but visitors have reported sunrises and sunsets that will take your breath away.

Best Time to Visit: The summer will have the warmest temperatures to enjoy water activities, but it will also be the busiest season.

Pass/Permit/Fees: There is a $5 fee to enter the park.

Closest City or Town: Caballo

Address: Highway 187, Caballo, NM 87931

GPS Coordinates: 32.9257° N, 107.2961° W

Did You Know? Sierra County is also home to New Mexico's largest body of water, Elephant Butte Lake. Elephant Butte Lake sits on a 40,000-acre park and has opportunities for hiking, camping, and some of New Mexico's best fishing. If you're interested in fishing for record-sized black, white, and striped bass, then this may be the destination for you. If you are only visiting the area for a few days and don't have your own boat, there are several places that will rent them out for the day.

Capulin Volcano National Monument

If you've ever wanted to explore an extinct volcano, here's your chance. Capulin Volcano National Monument is part of an 8,000-square-mile volcanic field known as Raton-Clayton. Visitors can hike on the paved Crater Rim Trail or go on the more strenuous trails that wrap around the base of Capulin. Additionally, you can go during Saturday nights in the summer to the Dark Sky stargazing events.

Best Time to Visit: The park is open year-round, but the summertime will likely be the busiest. You can also go to the overflow parking lot to view the night sky.

Pass/Permit/Fees: The park charges a $20 entrance fee per vehicle.

Closest City or Town: Capulin

Address: 46 Volcano, Capulin, NM 88414

GPS Coordinates: 36.7811° N, 103.9695° W

Did You Know? The Capulin Volcano has intrigued people from far and wide to explore the interesting crater, traveling by horse, wagon, car, or foot just to see it for themselves. Many notable people have historical connections to Capulin, such as Ernest Thompson Seton, the founder of the Boy Scouts of America, and Jessie Foote Jack, the first female custodian in the National Park Service.

Carlsbad Caverns

Carlsbad Caverns National Park is nestled in the Guadalupe Mountains of New Mexico. This spot is full of rocky slopes, deep canyons, and underground caves that are waiting to be explored.

Carlsbad Cavern is actually a fossilized limestone reef that was part of an inland sea that existed about 265 million years ago. Additionally, Indigenous Americans lived within the Guadalupe Mountains, and the remains of their cooking rings and pictographs can be found around the park boundaries.

Best Time to Visit: Carlsbad Caverns has warm weather year-round and almost always sunshine. However, the best time to visit is in October and November.

Pass/Permit/Fees: Permits to hike and camp in the backcountry are free, but visitors should get their permits ahead of time. Research, events, and cave exploration require a permit.

Closest City or Town: Carlsbad

Address: 727 Carlsbad Caverns Highway, Carlsbad, NM 88220

GPS Coordinates: 32.1291° N, 104.5539° W

Did You Know? The museum within the park has over a million cultural artifacts that are currently being preserved.

Guadalupe Backcountry Scenic Byway

The Guadalupe Backcountry Scenic Byway is a 30-mile road that goes west from the Chihuahuan Desert to the Guadalupe Escarpment. While driving on this scenic byway, visitors will see the vast deserts littered with cactus and dense pines. Not only that, but you may see mule deer, pronghorn antelope, gray fox, scaled quail, mourning dove, songbirds, and other small mammals.

Best Time to Visit: The scenic byway is open year-round, so you can drive this gorgeous road any time of year and remain comfortable in your temperature-controlled car. Try driving on the road at sunrise or sunset to get the most spectacular views. Always check the weather for storms so that you can make the most of your drive.

Pass/Permit/Fees: There are no fees to use the scenic byway.

Closest City or Town: Carlsbad

Address: Carlsbad Chamber of Commerce/Visitor Center, 302 S. Canal, Carlsbad, NM 88220

GPS Coordinates: 32.51512778° N, 104.3798425° W

Did You Know? There are many attractions to stop and visit along the drive, such as the Carlsbad Caverns and Lechugilla Cave. There are also trails for hiking, backpacking, camping, mountain biking, caving, and more.

Living Desert State Park

As its name suggests, Living Desert State Park is a living museum supporting a wealth of various plants and animals. The self-guided tour is approximately 1.3 miles and takes about an hour and a half to complete. While on the tour, visitors will see hundreds of succulents, sand dunes, and mountainous views. The park has several attractions, such as Birds to Bison, Never Cry Wolf and the Green House.

The Living Desert is modeled after the Chihuahuan Desert, which covers around 250,000 square miles. This desert is unique because about 9,000 years ago, the area was wet and covered in thick forests. When it started to dry, some plant species adapted, and others went extinct. This led to the unique plants that are seen in the desert today.

Best Time to Visit: The park is open year-round, but many people visit in late spring through fall for the best weather. However, it can be hot during the summer, and thunderstorms may occur.

Pass/Permit/Fees: The entrance fee is $5 per vehicle.

Closest City or Town: Carlsbad

Address: 1504 Skyline Road, Carlsbad, NM 88220

GPS Coordinates: 32.4419° N, 104.2781° W

Did You Know? The park features over 40 native animal species in its indoor-and-outdoor living museum.

Sitting Bull Falls

Sitting Bull Falls is a series of waterfalls, streams, and pools located in Lincoln National Forest. Once the water leaves the falls, it disappears between the gravel, cracks, and rocks, then reappears further downstream or becomes part of the Pecos Valley underground water reserve. This 150-foot-tall waterfall is a rare find in an arid desert, and the recreation area offers cool pools, pavilions, picnic areas, charcoal grills, and many outdoor activities such as hiking, biking, and horseback riding. There is a paved trail that leads to the falls as well as 16 miles of canyon trails for all outdoor activities.

Best Time to Visit: The busiest season for Sitting Bull Falls is the summer, but the mildest weather is in the spring and fall.

Pass/Permit/Fees: The fee to enter Sitting Bull Falls Recreation Area is $5 per vehicle.

Closest City or Town: Carlsbad

Address: 5203 Buena Vista Drive, Carlsbad, NM 88220

GPS Coordinates: 32.2432° N, 104.6963° W

Did You Know? While no one knows exactly how Sitting Bull Falls got its name, it's suspected that the falls are named after the well-known Sioux medicine man. However, the Apache tribes named the area *gostahanagunti*, which translates to "hidden gulf."

Cumbres & Toltec Scenic Railway

Visitors can experience an authentic steam train ride through the wilderness and across the steep mountain canyons of New Mexico's landscape. Traveling at a top speed of 12 miles per hour, you'll have time to see the plentiful wildlife along the route and catch your breath after viewing some of the most picturesque scenery in the West. You'll even enjoy a hot meal during the trip, which is included in your ticket price. The railroad was originally built in 1880 as a narrow-gauge extension of the Rio Grande and was designed to serve the silver mining communities of the San Juan Mountains in southwestern Colorado. The railroad converted its tracks to standard gauge in 1890 because of the difficulty of interchanging cars with other railroads.

Best Time to Visit: Full excursion trips begin at 8:30 a.m. and 10:00 a.m. daily. Half-day trips leave at 11:10 a.m. and 1:00 p.m. daily.

Pass/Permit/Fees: The price to visit the Cumbres & Toltec Scenic Railway depends on the car and trip length you choose. Check the website for pricing details.

Closest City or Town: Chama

How to get there: 500 Terrace Avenue, Chama, NM 87520

GPS Coordinates: 36.90413° N, 106.57811° W

Did You Know? The Cumbres & Toltec Scenic Railway is seen in several movies, including *Indiana Jones & The Last Crusade* and *A Million Ways to Die in the Wests*.

Ah-Shi-Sle-Pah Wilderness

The Ah-Shi-Sle-Pah Wilderness is a badlands area full of clay hills situated in the northeastern part of New Mexico. Because of its water-carved hills, the Ah-Shi-Sle-Pah Wilderness does not have much vegetation. Full of spectacular geological structures and formations, this area is home to many fossils. Even though there are no established trails in the Ah-Shi-Sle-Pah Wilderness, you can still pull your car over on the side of the road and experience the rolling hills, Great Basin scrubland, and grasslands for yourself.

Best Time to Visit: You can visit the wilderness area year-round, but the summer will have the warmest temperatures.

Pass/Permit/Fees: There are no fees to hike in the wilderness area.

Closest City or Town: Farmington

Address: 6251 College Boulevard, Farmington, NM 87402

GPS Coordinates: 36.13993° N, 107.92071° W

Did You Know? Ah-Shi-Sle-Pah means "gray salt," likely named because of its eroded badlands, vegetation-free area, and the fact that much of the area looks like gray rock. The Ah-Shi-Sle-Pah Wilderness boasts truly unique geological formations and fossils. While you are hiking around, it's not uncommon for you to see hoodoos, petrified logs, and stumps.

Bisti/De-Na Zin Badlands

The Bisti Badlands is about 60 square miles of remote landscapes and badlands. Nature has truly shaped the structures of Bisti/De-Na-Zin Badlands in a way that makes visitors think they've entered a completely new world. The rock formations are made of interbedded sandstone, shale, mudstone, coal, and silt. These form pinnacles, spires, cap rocks, and other breathtaking and seemingly impossible shapes. This wilderness area offers camping, rock climbing, mountain biking, hiking, horseback riding, and beautiful scenery. Visitors may even have the opportunity to identify fossils and petrified wood.

Best Time to Visit: The park is open year-round, but most visitors come in the late spring and fall to enjoy the best weather.

Pass/Permit/Fees: There are no fees to enter the park, but permits are required for scenic research and commercial guiding.

Closest City or Town: Farmington

Address: 6251 College Boulevard, Farmington, NM 87402

GPS Coordinates: 36.2921° N, 108.1298° W

Did You Know? The "Bisti Beast" is a fossil of an early ancestral relative of the *Tyrannosaurus rex*—the *Bistahiaversor Sealey*. The fossil was found by Paul Sealey in 1997. This 30-foot-tall dinosaur lived around 74 million years ago and to this day has only ever been found in New Mexico.

B-Square Ranch

The B-Square Ranch is a working farm and ranch that is also home to two museums and seven man-made lakes. It is the winter home to over 115,000 waterfowl. Abundant populations of deer, quail, hawks, pheasant, eagles, owls, pigeons, sheep, turkeys, and cattle roam across the ranch's 75 acres. The Bolack Museum of Fish and Wildlife features one of the largest private collections of specimens, and the Bolack Electromechanical Museum features a 40-year collection of antique electrical, communication, radio, agricultural, and industrial artifacts on permanent display. Since the ranch is a working operation, it makes an ideal natural laboratory for both children and adults. Learning opportunities in environmental education are readily available, and more than 100,000 people visit the ranch to take advantage of these opportunities each year.

Best Time to Visit: The B-Square Ranch is open Monday through Saturday from 9:00 a.m. to 3:00 p.m.

Pass/Permit/Fees: There is no fee to visit the B-Square Ranch.

Closest City or Town: Farmington

Address: 3901 Bloomfield Highway, Farmington, NM 87401

GPS Coordinates: 36.71604° N, 108.16152° W

Did You Know? The B-Square Ranch was the site of the television movie *Coyote Mountain*, which was filmed in 2010 and featured actors Drew Scott and Jackie Blackmore.

Chaco Culture National Historical Park

Chaco Culture National Historical Park features many self-guided tours of cultural and natural sites, including Una Vida, Hungo Pavi, Pueblo Bonito, Chetro Ketl, Pueblo del Arroyo, and Casa Rinconada. The park has many nature trails for hiking. You'll see ancient roads, petroglyphs, stairways, and overlooks of the valley.

This historical site has massive cultural significance. Chaco Canyon has more than 4,000 prehistoric and historic archaeological sites. Some of these sites preserve early civilization, 16 great houses, prehistoric trade networks, and more.

Best Time to Visit: While the park is open year-round, the best times to visit are the spring and fall because of the moderate temperatures. The summers reach 80°F to 90°F, and the winters may have nights that dip below freezing.

Pass/Permit/Fees: It costs $25 for a vehicle to enter the park, $20 for a motorcycle, and $15 for an individual.

Closest City or Town: Farmington

Address: Farmington Convention & Visitors Bureau, 3041 E. Main Street, Farmington, NM 87402

GPS Coordinates: 36.0530° N, 107.9559° W

Did You Know? Chaco Culture National Historical Park showcases more than 10,000 years of human history.

Four Corners Monument

The Four Corners Monument marks the only place in the country where four states meet: New Mexico, Arizona, Colorado, and Utah. The monument exists on rural Navajo land, so there are no accommodations within 30 miles. There is, however, a newly redesigned Navajo vendor market where visitors can purchase authentic native artwork and crafts. The monument allows visitors to be in four states at one time by putting each hand and foot in a different state. Additionally, the monument marks the boundary between the Navajo Nation and the Ute Mountain Ute Tribe Reservation. People have been traveling to the Four Corners Monument since at least 1908 to take photographs of family and friends stretching themselves across four states.

Best Time to Visit: From October 1 to March 31, the Four Corners Monument is open daily from 8:00 a.m. to 4:45 p.m. The rest of the year, it is open daily from 8:00 a.m. to 5:45 p.m.

Pass/Permit/Fees: The fee to visit Four Corners Monument is $5 per person.

Closest City or Town: Farmington

Address: Farmington Convention & Visitor's Bureau, 3041 E. Main Street, Farmington, NM 87402

GPS Coordinates: 36.99994° N, 109.04539° W

Did You Know? The state border lines placed in 1931 on an elevated concrete pad surrounding a brass marker were not added until 1992.

Shiprock Peak

Shiprock Peak is a towering volcanic rock formation that summits at 7,178 feet above sea level. At the center of three separate volcanic pressure ridges, this geological feature is truly a sight. This rock formation is sacred to the Navajo people and is known in the Navajo language as *Tsé Bit' a'i*, meaning "rock with wings." Hiking or climbing Shiprock is not allowed because it is sacred ground, but you can still get picturesque views of the structure from a nearby dirt road.

Best Time to Visit: You can visit the structure year-round from the paved roads with views of the structure.

Pass/Permit/Fees: No fees are required to visit Shiprock Peak.

Closest City or Town: Farmington

Address: Farmington Convention & Visitor's Bureau, 3041 E. Main Street, Farmington, NM 87402

GPS Coordinates: 36.7856° N, 108.6870° W

Did You Know? If you want to walk in the footsteps of some of your favorite actors, make sure to visit Shiprock Peak. This rock formation has made appearances in movies such as *Transformers* (2007), *John Carter* (2012), *Natural Born Killers* (1994), *The Host* (2013), *The Lone Ranger* (2013), *Jumanji: The Next Level* (2019), and others.

Folsom Falls

Folsom Falls is one of three small waterfalls that are part of the Dry Cimarron River. They are currently located on private land, and visitors are warned not to trespass. For years, the area was open to the public, but it is now managed and leased by New Mexico Fish and Wildlife. If you take the Dry Cimarron Scenic Byway, you'll eventually come across Folsom Falls. There is a small area for parking off the side of the road, and you'll have to get through the gates to reach the falls. From the gate, they are only a couple of hundred yards away.

Best Time to Visit: Available to be viewed year-round, the best time to visit would be during New Mexico's hot summer.

Pass/Permit/Fees: There are no fees to get to the falls, but the falls are currently on private land owned by New Mexico Fish and Wildlife.

Closest City or Town: Folsom

Address: Folsom Museum and Visitor Center, Junction of Highways 325 & 456, Folsom, NM 88419

GPS Coordinates: 36.8728° N, 103.8808° W

Did You Know? Folsom Falls is a favorite fishing spot and scenic picnicking area. While the falls themselves aren't huge, they still offer the beautiful sound of rushing water. However, it's not recommended to swim at Folsom Falls because the current can get too strong.

Billy the Kid Museum

Museum originator Ed Sweet began collecting items related to Billy the Kid when he was a peddler going from house to house selling apples, sweet potatoes, and handmade brooms and mattresses. Occasionally, people were willing to trade old items for his wares, and he accepted numerous Billy the Kid artifacts as payment. Sweet and his wife, Jewel, opened a one-building museum dedicated to their collection in 1953. Since then, the museum has become known around the world for its collection of 60,000 items, most of which have significant historical value. The museum continues to be operated by the Sweet family, with Donald Sweet taking over the museum in 1979.

Best Time to Visit: The Billy the Kid Museum is open daily from May 15 through October 1 from 8:30 a.m. to 5:00 p.m. From October 2 to May 14, the museum is closed on Sunday.

Pass/Permit/Fees: Admission is $5 for adults, $4 for seniors ages 62 and older, and $3 for children ages 7 to 15. Children ages six and under are free.

Closest City or Town: Fort Sumner

Address: 1435 E. Sumner Avenue, Fort Sumner, NM 88119

GPS Coordinates: 34.46717° N, 104.22933° W

Did You Know? Billy the Kid frequently visited Fort Sumner and was killed in the town in 1881 by Lincoln County Sheriff Pat Garrett.

Catwalk Trail Falls

Catwalk Trail Falls goes along an 1890s mining waterway and traverses through many historical sites. Part of the Gila National Forest, the entrance to the Catwalk Trail is also called Catwalk National Recreation #207 Trail. The trail goes for about 1.5 miles, featuring hidden pools and gorgeous waterfalls, and leads to the more rigorous trails of the Gila Wilderness.

Best Time to Visit: The most popular time to visit is during the summer, but the mildest weather will be in the spring and fall. Before you go, however, check with the U.S. Forest Service for weather and trail conditions to make sure it's safe. The trail is typically open from dawn to dusk, but it can also be heavily used during popular hiking times.

Pass/Permit/Fees: There is a $3 parking fee to hike the Catwalk Trail.

Closest City or Town: Glenwood

Address: 18 Ranger Station Road, Glenwood, NM 88039

GPS Coordinates: 33.3725° N 108.8417° W

Did You Know? The Catwalk was originally named for the plank-board walkway on top of the steel pipe that once brought water down to an ore-processing plant. Even though nearly all the pipe is now gone, most of the modern hiking trail follows the same route. So, while you're hiking, keep an eye out for the remains of the old pipe.

El Morro National Monument

Even though El Morro National Monument is one of New Mexico's smaller national parks, it holds several wonders, beautiful landscapes, and major historical context. You can visit Inscription Rock, the site of over 2,000 drawings that have been inscribed in the sandstone, or see the pool that makes this area so unique. There are two major trails in the park: the Inscription Trail and the Headland Trail. The Inscription Trail heads towards Inscription Rock and the pool, and the Headland Trail explores the volcanic craters of the El Malpais area, El Morro Valley, and the ancient ruins of Astinna.

Best Time to Visit: The park is open year-round, but the summer is the most popular time to visit.

Pass/Permit/Fees: There is no fee to enter the park.

Closest City or Town: Grants

Address: Mile Marker 44.6, Highway 53, Ramah, NM 87321

GPS Coordinates: 35.0396° N, 108.3451° W

Did You Know? El Morro is full of sandstone cliffs that hide a deep pool of water. This oasis has been a focal point of weary travels for thousands of years because the pool holds water year-round. Many of these travelers have left their mark on the area via inscriptions in the colorful stone.

Soda Dam

The Soda Dam is a 7,000year-old natural bridge made from calcium carbonate. This odd geographic structure is actually a hot-springs deposit, and before State Route 4 was built, it was getting bigger every year. Unfortunately, the road destroyed part of the dam and re-routed its natural water flow, so the dam is slowly disintegrating. However, that does not stop visitors from visiting this 300-foot-long, 50-foot-tall natural dam.

Best Time to Visit: You can visit the Soda Dam any time of year. However, the best driving conditions are in the late spring through fall.

Pass/Permit/Fees: There are currently no fees to visit this geological structure.

Closest City or Town: Jemez Springs

Address: Walatowa Visitor Center, 7413 Highway 4, Jemez Pueblo, NM 87024

GPS Coordinates: 35.7920° N, 106.6866° W

Did You Know? The substance that makes up the Soda Dam, calcium carbonate, is the same substance that is found in eggshells, snail shells, and pearls. It's a very common mineral that is naturally found in limestone, calcite, and aragonite. In fact, it makes up 4 percent of the earth's crust. Additionally, calcium carbonate can be used as chalk for writing purposes, as a dietary supplement, and as an antacid to relieve stomach pain.

Spence Hot Springs

Spence Hot Springs is a small pool located in the Santa Fe National Forest. The springs maintain a temperature of 95°F in the springtime, and even though the temperature remains close to that of the human body, the pool will feel heavenly on a chilly spring, fall, or winter day. Visitors can hike an easy trail to the springs. The Spence Hot Springs Trailhead is rated for all skill levels, so every visitor can enjoy the gorgeous scenic views and then soak in the springs.

Best Time to Visit: While the busiest season is in the summer, the best time to visit the hot springs is in the fall and winter.

Pass/Permit/Fees: No passes are required to hike to the hot springs.

Closest City or Town: Jemez Springs

Address: E. State Highway 4, Jemez Springs, NM 87025

GPS Coordinates: 35.8495° N, 106.6298° W

Did You Know? Hot springs are heated by geothermal heat from inside the earth's crust. In areas where volcanos once erupted, the springs are heated by subsurface magma that heats groundwater and produces steam. In areas with no volcanic activity, the temperature of the rocks under the spring will get warmer as they become closer to the earth's interior (i.e., the deeper the rocks, the warmer they are). This is known as the geothermal gradient.

Valles Caldera National Preserve

The Valles Caldera is a 13-mile-wide depression in the earth that was caused by a massive volcanic eruption. This volcano erupted nearly 1.25 million years ago, and since then, the area has become full of mountain meadows, trickling springs, and an abundance of wildlife. The 88,900-acre preserve offers several outdoor activities, such as fishing, hiking, horseback riding, mountain biking, and astronomy. You can also look for the preserve's 51 mammal species, 117 bird species, and different types of reptiles, amphibians, and fish.

Best Time to Visit: The park is open year-round, but the summer is the most popular time to visit the preserve.

Pass/Permit/Fees: A 7-day pass is $25 per vehicle.

Closest City or Town: Jemez Springs

Address: 39201 New Mexico Highway 4, Jemez Springs, NM 87025

GPS Coordinates: 35.8321° N, 106.4870° W

Did You Know? Native Americans traversed the land of Valles Caldera National Preserve for thousands of years. Not only did they hunt, fish, and gather food, but the area was also known for its obsidian, a substance used to craft many ancient tools.

Art Obscura

This art museum is one of several facilities located in an art compound in Mesilla Park. Art Obscura was founded by Deret Roberts in 2013, and since then, it has represented more than 100 local artists. It specializes in uncommon artwork, such as vintage guitars, snakes in jars, hand-painted signs, and even oil paintings with interesting themes. There is a new exhibition every month, which is installed every second Saturday of each month in the main gallery. Various antiques are also on display throughout the museum, particularly upstairs from the main gallery. There are also one-day pop-up shows that are sprinkled into the rotation throughout the year. Artwork from previous exhibitions and local artists, antiques, and other gifts can be purchased from the gift shop located on the premises or from the museum's website.

Best Time to Visit: Art Obscura is open Thursday through Saturday from 10:00 a.m. to 7:00 p.m. and Sunday from 11:00 a.m. to 3:00 p.m.

Pass/Permit/Fees: There is no fee to visit Art Obscura.

Closest City or Town: Las Cruces

Address: 3206 Harrelson Street, Las Cruces, NM 88005

GPS Coordinates: 32.27658° N, 106.76796° W

Did You Know? Local artists such as Jess Reinhard and Christina Ballew have had displays at Art Obscura, and their original art pieces are for sale in the museum's store.

Bar Canyon-Soledad Canyon Waterfall

For gorgeous views of the Organ Mountains and Mesilla Valley, hike the 3-mile loop of the Bar Canyon Trail. Depending on how much rainfall there's been, the waterfall you'll pass on the trail can range from a slight trickle to a massive stream that runs into a small pond. To get to the waterfall, you will have to deviate from the main trail, but it's not a far walk. You can hike, bike, or travel the trail by horseback, and the Soledad Canyon Lookout is known for its wildlife-viewing opportunities.

Best Time to Visit: While the park is open year-round, the best times to visit are during the spring and fall because they're likely to be the driest and mildest seasons. However, the summer is also a popular time to hike to see the waterfall.

Pass/Permit/Fees: There are no fees to hike the trails.

Closest City or Town: Las Cruces

Address: 1330 Soledad Canyon Road, Las Cruces, NM 88011

GPS Coordinates: 32.306° N, 106.589° W

Did You Know? If you take a slight detour off the trail, you will find the remains of a 20th-century homestead. The ruins have been abandoned for nearly 100 years, but the foundation stands to mark its location. Even though the structure is manmade, nature has reclaimed much of it over time.

Black Box Theatre

The Black Box Theatre is home to the No Strings Theatre Company, a community-based nonprofit organization committed to presenting contemporary or lesser-known theater productions to the Las Cruces community. This group provides opportunities for local playwrights to create new plays. The Black Box Theatre was built especially for the No Strings Theatre Company in 2000. Instead of a ground-breaking ceremony, the theatre company had a string-cutting one. Local community members tied strings from various locations across the globe (the furthest location represented by a string was Sweden) to the chain-link fence that surrounded the construction site. The strings were then cut during the ceremony.

Best Time to Visit: The best time to visit the Black Box Theatre is when there is a show playing that you want to see. Visit the theatre's website for showtimes and dates.

Pass/Permit/Fees: The fee to visit the Black Box Theatre depends on show and seat selection. Visit the theatre's website for pricing details.

Closest City or Town: Las Cruces

Address: 430 N. Main Street, Las Cruces, NM 88001

GPS Coordinates: 32.31358° N, 106.77951° W

Did You Know? The first production at the Black Box Theatre was Edward Albee's *Seascape*.

Branigan Cultural Center

The Branigan Cultural Center is housed in a 1935 Pueblo Revival-style structure that was once the home of the first library in Las Cruces. It is committed to engaging guests in the rich history and culture of the Southwest through artistic, historical, and cultural exhibitions and programs. Recently, the center was closed for renovations but reopened in September 2021 with new floors throughout the 1,500-square-foot building, energy-efficient lighting, repainted walls, and other improvements. The first exhibit in the newly renovated space is *Cleared for Take Off: Aviation in Southern New Mexico*, which features "an exploration of the history of aviation from its introduction in 1916 through the post-WWII civilian flying boom and into the 21st century."

Best Time to Visit: The Branigan Cultural Center is open Tuesday through Friday from 10:00 a.m. to 4:30 p.m. and Saturday from 9:00 a.m. to 4:30 p.m. It is open until 8:00 p.m. on Thursdays.

Pass/Permit/Fees: There is no fee to visit the Branigan Cultural Center unless you're attending a paid show or production.

Closest City or Town: Las Cruces

Address: 501 N. Main Street, Las Cruces, NM 88001

GPS Coordinates: 32.31407° N, 106.77961° W

Did You Know? The Branigan Cultural Center is not a collecting institution but does host a permanent history exhibit.

Dripping Springs Natural Area

With more than 4 miles of easy hiking paths, including the Dripping Springs Trail, the Dripping Springs Natural Area also features fantastic wildlife-viewing opportunities and an excellent Visitor Center that provides interpretive displays of the Organ Mountains. Wildlife that you can expect to see include red-tailed hawks, golden eagles, Gambel's quails, rock squirrels, desert mule deer, coyotes, black-throated sparrows, cactus wrens, desert cottontails, and tree lizards, among others. The Dripping Springs Trail takes visitors to a spectacular waterfall and the remains of an abandoned mountain camp. As you hike along this trail, you'll be following the path that was created by stagecoaches many decades earlier.

Best Time to Visit: The best time to visit Dripping Springs Natural Area is during the spring, summer, or fall when the weather is best.

Pass/Permit/Fees: There is a $5 fee per vehicle per day to visit Dripping Springs Natural Area.

Closest City or Town: Las Cruces

Address: 15000 Dripping Springs Road, Las Cruces, NM 88005

GPS Coordinates: 32.33044° N, 106.59045° W

Did You Know? The 3-mile La Cueva Loop Trail ends at a cave that can be traced back to 5000 BCE. It was once home to Giovanni Maria Agostini, also referred to as the Hermit. He lived in the cave until he was killed in the 1860s.

Fillmore Waterfall New Mexico

The Fillmore Waterfall is 40 feet tall and found at an elevation of 6,240 feet above sea level. During the winter and early spring, the waterfall flows heavily, but during the summer, you may get to see the remnants of the slow trickle and pool that is left over from the snowmelt. The waterfall is found in the spectacular Organ Mountains. While on the Fillmore Canyon Trail, you'll see old mining shafts, gorgeous views of the canyon, creeks, and plenty of flora and fauna.

Best Time to Visit: The trails are open year-round, but if you want to see heavy water flow and a frothy waterfall, it's best to go in early spring or during the winter. Keep in mind that the trails are only open from 8:00 a.m. until 5:00 p.m.

Pass/Permit/Fees: There is a $3 fee for a single-day pass for one vehicle.

Closest City or Town: Las Cruces

Address: Las Cruces Visitor Center, 211 N. Water Street, Las Cruces, NM 88001

GPS Coordinates: 32.3386° N, 106.5999° W

Did You Know? There were many silver and lead mining camps located in the Organ Mountains from 1849 to 1898. In 1898, the Modoc Mining Company invested nearly $1 million in creating a 3-story mill that had many shafts, hoists, and tramways. Unfortunately, the mine went bankrupt in 1903 due to a lack of water and other issues.

La Llorona Park

Located in the heart of Las Cruces, La Llorona Park offers a multi-use path that follows the Rio Grande River. At times, the Rio Grande is dammed in this area, so the path leads past a dry riverbed, but in the summer, the water is released to provide irrigation to the farms along the river. Many residents use La Llorona Park as a place for recreation in the warmer months. Swimming, kayaking, and tubing are all popular water activities. The multi-use path is accessible at Run Along Road and connects with the Outfall Channel Trail. La Llorona Park acts as a trailhead since it has free parking. The path heads out of the park, and the paved trail continues south before concluding at a small parking lot near Calle Del Norte.

Best Time to Visit: The best time to visit La Llorona Park is in the summer when the Rio Grande waters are near the park and available for many water activities.

Pass/Permit/Fees: There is no fee to visit La Llorona Park.

Closest City or Town: Las Cruces

Address: 3440 W. Picacho Avenue, Las Cruces, NM 88007

GPS Coordinates: 32.31142° N, 106.82722° W

Did You Know? Be aware that in the late summer and early fall, the monsoon rains may cause flooding in the park and across the path. Use caution when walking or riding during this time of the year.

Las Cruces Railroad Museum

Situated in a historic depot that once belonged to the Atchison, Topeka, and Santa Fe Railway, the Las Cruces Railroad Museum celebrates the history of the railroad in Las Cruces and the impact it had on southern New Mexico. Model trains, railroading tools, photographs, artifacts, text panels, and railroad memorabilia are all on display. Lectures, classes, and kids' activities are also available to visitors. One of the three model train layouts can be run by the public. The museum hosts two major annual events: the Old-Fashioned Holiday Display, which is held on the first Friday of December from 5:00 p.m. to 8:00 p.m., and Railroad Days, which is held the week of National Train Day in May.

Best Time to Visit: The Las Cruces Railroad Museum is open Tuesday through Friday from 10:00 a.m. to 4:30 p.m. and Saturday from 9:00 a.m. to 4:30 p.m.

Pass/Permit/Fees: There is no fee to visit the Las Cruces Railroad Museum.

Closest City or Town: Las Cruces

Address: 351 N. Mesilla Street, Las Cruces, NM 88005

GPS Coordinates: 32.30977° N, 106.78677° W

Did You Know? Railroads didn't reach New Mexico until 1879, a decade after the Atchison, Topeka, and Santa Fe Railway were founded. The railroad initially targeted Mesilla, but the residents didn't want to give up their land for it to be built. Las Cruces was chosen as an alternate option since it was only 3 miles from Mesilla.

Mesilla Valley Bosque State Park

On the banks of the Rio Grande, the Mesilla Valley Bosque State Park serves as a preserve that provides a temporary stopover for thousands of migratory birds. The river woodlands and wetlands offer visitors many opportunities to view wildlife in their natural environments while walking along one of several self-guided nature trails. You can also request a ranger-led tour if you prefer. The park is located at an elevation of 3,879 feet and, as such, provides spectacular views, intriguing geology, fly-fishing opportunities, and equestrian trails. The park is an Audubon-designated Important Birding Area, and it's stop number 43 along the Statewide Birding Trail.

Best Time to Visit: The best time to visit the Mesilla Valley Bosque State Park is during spring, summer, or fall when the weather is best.

Pass/Permit/Fees: There is a $5 fee per vehicle per day to visit the Mesilla Valley Bosque State Park.

Closest City or Town: Las Cruces

Address: 5000 Calle de Norte, Mesilla, NM 88046

GPS Coordinates: 32.26051° N, 106.82373° W

Did You Know? The park is located at the crossroads of the river forest and the Chihuahuan Desert, which forms an "ecotone" that features plants and wildlife native to both ecological regions. It also protects one of the last remaining Rio Grande bosques in New Mexico.

New Mexico Farm and Ranch Heritage Museum

The New Mexico Farm and Ranch Heritage Museum is an interactive facility that celebrates the 4,000-year history of farming and ranching in the state. With more than 24,000 square feet of exhibit space, visitors are able to see corrals filled with livestock, watch farming-related demonstrations, and enjoy several landscaped gardens. Exhibits include *Her Land: Women in Agriculture*, *Home on the Range: From Ranches to Rockets*, *Farm Life in New Mexico: Then & Now*, and several others. The mission of the museum is to connect "the present generation to the history of farming and ranching in New Mexico."

Best Time to Visit: The New Mexico Farm and Ranch Heritage Museum is open Monday through Saturday from 10:00 a.m. to 4:00 p.m.

Pass/Permit/Fees: Admission is $5 for adults, $3 for children ages 4 to 17, $4 for seniors ages 60 and older, and $2 for military personnel and veterans. Children ages three and under are free.

Closest City or Town: Las Cruces

Address: 4100 Dripping Springs Road, Las Cruces, NM 88011

GPS Coordinates: 32.30050° N, 106.72096° W

Did You Know? The livestock corrals on the South 20 are home to seven breeds of cattle.

Rio Grande Vineyard & Winery

The Rio Grande Vineyard & Winery is located in the heart of the Mesilla Valley, which is one of the oldest winemaking regions in the United States. In fact, Spanish priests began making wine in the area in the early 1600s. The winery opened in 2004, and it boasts a spectacular view of the Organ Mountains. The 28-acre estate vineyards are responsible for delicious wine varieties like Petit Verdot, El Santo, Land of Manana, Desert Nights Rose, Flor Blanca, and several others. The vineyards grow 12 grape varietals, from which 90 percent of the wines are made. To broaden their offerings, the winery trades grapes with other New Mexico vineyards, but all wines are produced in an on-site facility, which can be viewed from the tasting room.

Best Time to Visit: The Rio Grande Vineyard & Winery is open Wednesday and Thursday from 3:00 p.m. to 8:00 p.m., Friday and Saturday from 12:00 p.m. to 9:00 p.m., and Sunday from 12:00 p.m. to 8:00 p.m.

Pass/Permit/Fees: There is no fee to visit the Rio Grande Vineyard & Winery but bring some money to sample the wines.

Closest City or Town: Las Cruces

Address: 5321 N. Highway 28, Las Cruces, NM 88005

GPS Coordinates: 32.23471° N, 106.76044° W

Did You Know? The Rio Grande Vineyard & Winery produces between 5,000 and 10,000 gallons of wine each year and uses between 35 and 40 tons of grapes.

Soledad Canyon

For gorgeous views of the Organ Mountains and the Southern Mesilla Valley, you can't do much better than Soledad Canyon, located just 10 miles outside of Las Cruces. There are several trails leading from this day-use area that are perfect for hiking, mountain biking, and equestrian use. The trails are rated between easy and rugged, so there's something for everyone, regardless of age or ability. The 3.3-mile Soledad Canyon Loop trail features a waterfall and gorgeous views of the canyon itself. It's a popular, dog-friendly trail. This loop is also accessible year-round, which makes it a favorite of locals who want to hike during any season. In the summer, there are plenty of shady spots along the trail, and some of the trails are even wheelchair accessible.

Best Time to Visit: The best time to visit Soledad Canyon is during the spring, summer, or fall when the weather is warmest.

Pass/Permit/Fees: There are no fees to visit Soledad Canyon.

Closest City or Town: Las Cruces

Address: 13300 Soledad Canyon Road, Las Cruces, NM 88011

GPS Coordinates: 32.30542° N, 106.59382° W

Did You Know? The Soledad Canyon Day Use Area is located at the junction of Soledad Canyon and Bar Canyon, and various trails will take visitors through one or the other.

Zuhl Museum

The Zuhl Museum on the campus of New Mexico State University (NMSU) is part art gallery and part natural history museum. It has more than 1,800 specimens of fossils, minerals, and petrified wood. One of five NMSU museums, the Zuhl Museum is named for Herb and Joan Zuhl, who saw a rancher in Arizona remove a petrified log from his land and decided to dig up a log and ship it home to New York City. For more than three decades, the Zuhls have been collecting minerals, fossils, and petrified wood for their own collection, but when they retired in 1991, they moved 2,000 of their most impressive specimens to Las Cruces, where they decided to make their retirement home. In 2000, the Zuhls underwrote the cost of expanding gallery space to house their collection on the NMSU campus, and the museum opened in 2004.

Best Time to Visit: The Zuhl Museum is currently closed for renovations but will be open Tuesday through Friday and every second Saturday of the month from 12:00 p.m. to 4:00 p.m.

Pass/Permit/Fees: There is no fee to visit the Zuhl Museum.

Closest City or Town: Las Cruces

Address: 775 College Drive, Las Cruces, NM 88003

GPS Coordinates: 32.28258° N, 106.75938° W

Did You Know? The collection at the Zuhl Museum contains fossils from Wyoming, South Dakota, and Germany, and Morocco.

Continental Divide National Scenic Trail

The Continental Divide National Scenic Trail spans many states across the United States and follows the footsteps of ancient traders who traveled miles to sell their goods. There are 775 miles of completed trail systems in New Mexico that go through the Big Hatchet Mountains Wilderness, the Gila Wilderness, the Aldo Leopold Wilderness, El Malpais, the Rio Puerco, the Chama River, and San Pedro Parks Wilderness before diverging into the Rocky Mountains.

The trail goes through several different biospheres, from the cold tundra to the arid desert. There are many attractions and sites to explore along the way, and you may even encounter mountain lions, bears, and moose in this month-long backpacking experience.

Best Time to Visit: The best time to hike the Continental Divide is in the fall (mid-September/October/November). These will be the driest months and the safest to hike as there is little likelihood of rain.

Pass/Permit/Fees: No permits are required for much of the trail, but camping and hiking in state parks may require a permit.

Closest City or Town: Lordsburg

Address: Lordsburg Visitor Information Center, I-10 West Exit 20 Rest Area, Lordsburg, NM 88045

GPS Coordinates: 31.4970° N, 108.2087° W

Did You Know? The Continental Divide Trail, also known as the CDT, was first established by Congress in 1978 and spanned 3,100 miles across the United States.

Bandelier National Monument

With a plethora of wildlife and hiking trails for all abilities, the Bandelier National Monument is a great place for all to visit. There are over 70 miles of backpacking trails in the park that go through canyons and mesas.

Bandelier is home to many animals and a range of ecosystems. Visitors may see mule deer, bighorn sheep, mountain lions, black bears, bobcats, Abert's squirrels, lizards, rattlesnakes, and numerous year-round and migratory birds.

Best Time to Visit: The best time to visit is in the late spring and fall. You'll experience mild weather and minimal storms.

Pass/Permit/Fees: While some holidays will have free entrance days, Bandelier normally charges $25 per vehicle, $20 per motorcycle, or $15 per individual. A permit is required for overnight stays.

Closest City or Town: Los Alamos

Address: 15 Entrance Road, Los Alamos, NM 87544

GPS Coordinates: 35.7647° N, 106.3228° W

Did You Know? On warm fall days, you may see a tarantula crossing the path ahead of you, so make sure to bring your camera.

Bradbury Science Museum

Robert Krohn, the scientist in charge of early nuclear tests at the Los Alamos Scientific Laboratory, established the Bradbury Science Museum in 1953 to house research related to weapons artifacts. Krohn was able to convince the laboratory director at the time, Norris Bradbury, to create a museum in an old icehouse located on the bank of nearby Ashley Pond. The museum officially opened to the public in 1954. Due to the popularity of the museum, it was forced to relocate to a larger facility in 1993. A building located in downtown Los Alamos was chosen for the site and is still the museum's home today. There are approximately 60 interactive exhibits showcasing the history of the Manhattan Project and the laboratory's research.

Best Time to Visit: The Bradbury Science Museum is open Tuesday through Saturday from 11:00 a.m. to 4:00 p.m.

Pass/Permit/Fees: There is no fee to visit the Bradbury Science Museum.

Closest City or Town: Los Alamos

Address: 1350 Central Avenue, Los Alamos, NM 87544

GPS Coordinates: 35.88231° N, 106.29856° W

Did You Know? More than 80,000 people visit the Bradbury Science Museum each year, a number that has remained steady since the 1980s. Even in its first year, in 1954, the museum's intriguing subject and exhibits attracted 14,000 visitors from all 50 states and 40 countries.

Los Alamos Cooperative Market

The goal of the Los Alamos Cooperative Market is to provide the Los Alamos community with affordable, wholesome foods and other goods in a socially responsible, ecologically sustainable, and economically appropriate manner. The co-op emphasizes that food is for people, not for profit, and strives to maintain a high standard of quality products. The market is also designed to provide a sales outlet for northern New Mexico growers, producers, and vendors, who in turn provide fresh, locally grown or produced goods to the community and raise awareness about health, nutrition, and cooperative values. As a co-op, the market is "owned" by members who shop at the market and provide goods. It's managed by a board of directors and general manager, who continuously assess and respond to community needs.

Best Time to Visit: The Los Alamos Cooperative Market is open Monday through Sunday from 8:00 a.m. to 8:00 p.m.

Pass/Permit/Fees: There is no fee to visit the Los Alamos Cooperative Market but be sure to bring money for your purchases.

Closest City or Town: Los Alamos

Address: 95 Entrada Drive, Los Alamos, NM 87544

GPS Coordinates: 35.87763° N, 106.26106° W

Did You Know? Everyone can shop at the Los Alamos Cooperative Market, even if they're not a member.

Los Alamos History Museum

The Los Alamos History Museum is committed to presenting the stories of Los Alamos residents and events through historic buildings, documents, photographs, artifacts, audio recordings, video recordings, and interactive experiences. It was established by the Los Alamos Historical Society, an organization that is dedicated to preserving, promoting, and communicating the history of the community. The museum includes the Los Alamos Ranch School Guest Cottage, the Hans Bethe House, the Romero Cabin, and the Oppenheimer House, in addition to exhibits such as *Rock, Paper, Secrets!* Walking tours throughout the Los Alamos historical district and online virtual exhibits are also offered through the museum.

Best Time to Visit: The Los Alamos History Museum is open Monday through Friday from 9:00 a.m. to 5:00 p.m. and Saturday from 10:00 a.m. to 4:00 p.m.

Pass/Permit/Fees: Admission to the Los Alamos History Museum is $5.

Closest City or Town: Los Alamos

Address: 1050 Bathtub Row, Los Alamos, NM 87544

GPS Coordinates: 35.88332° N, 106.30241° W

Did You Know? The Los Alamos Ranch School Guest Cottage, where the Los Alamos History Museum is located, was initially built as an infirmary in 1918 during the Spanish Flu pandemic.

Manhattan Project National Historical Park

In the early 20th century, Los Alamos was chosen as the location for a secret laboratory where the world's first atomic weapons were designed and built. Located on top of a mesa and surrounded by canyons, the area was sufficiently remote, and the close proximity to Santa Fe gave workers easy access to resources and transportation. Many top scientists such as Dr. J. Robert Oppenheimer, Richard Feynman, Norris Bradbury, and Hans Bethe lived in Los Alamos while the Manhattan Project was underway. These scientists collaborated to create the theoretical and experimental tests that would lead to the first atomic weapons. The Los Alamos National Laboratory still exists on the site today, but the Visitor Center provides historical information about the Manhattan Project and the nearby Gun Site Facilities and V-Site Facilities.

Best Time to Visit: The Los Alamos Visitor Center is open Friday through Monday from 10:00 a.m. to 3:00 p.m.

Pass/Permit/Fees: There is no fee to visit the park.

Closest City or Town: Los Alamos

Address: Los Alamos Visitor Center, 475 20th Street, Suite A, Los Alamos, NM 87544

GPS Coordinates: 35.88160° N, 106.30207° W

Did You Know? The Manhattan Project National Park was only designated a national park in 2014.

Pajarito Mountain Ski Area

Located on the north face of Pajarito Mountain, the Pajarito Mountain Ski Area is a popular destination for both locals and out-of-state visitors. The ski season at this resort typically runs from late December to early April, but it will occasionally open in November if snow is abundant. In the summer, the ski area hosts various special events, many of which involve mountain biking. There is an extensive network of mountain bike trails that crisscross the mountain and one that takes bikers to the summit. There are also equestrian, and hiking trails leading from the ski area since horses and hikers should stay off the trails designated for bikes. This ski area originally opened in 1957 as a primitive ski facility, but a T-bar ski lift was installed in 1962, and the first chairlift was added in 1970.

Best Time to Visit: The best time to visit Pajarito Mountain Ski Area is between December and April for skiing.

Pass/Permit/Fees: The fee to visit Pajarito Mountain Ski Area varies depending on the date and event. Check the website for lift ticket and event pricing.

Closest City or Town: Los Alamos

Address: 397 Camp May Road, Los Alamos, NM 87544

GPS Coordinates: 35.89557° N, 106.39029° W

Did You Know? In Spanish, *pajarito* means "little bird." The name was inspired by Edgar Lee Hewett, an archeologist in the area who worked on the Tsirege site (*tsirege* means "bird place").

The Bathtub Row Brewing Co-Op

Located in downtown Los Alamos, the Bathtub Row Brewing Co-Op is a place where the community can gather and enjoy locally brewed beer. The environment is relaxed, comfortable, and designed to bring people together over a beer. The style is meant to evoke a small neighborhood pub in England, where the beer is brewed onsite and served as fresh as humanly possible. The taproom is family-friendly and open seven days a week to cater to any schedule. Beers on tap vary based on what's in season and what's ready to serve, but favorites include Barnicle Babes Belgian Dubbel, Wine Grape Wild Ale, and New Mexi Lager.

Best Time to Visit: The Bathtub Row Brewing Co-Op is open Monday through Thursday from 2:00 p.m. to 10:00 p.m. and Friday-Sunday from 12:00 p.m. to 10:00 p.m.

Pass/Permit/Fees: There is no fee to visit the Bathtub Row Brewing Co-Op but bring money to sample beer.

Closest City or Town: Los Alamos

Address: 163 Central Park Square, Los Alamos, NM 87544

GPS Coordinates: 35.88440° N, 106.30053° W

Did You Know? The Bathtub Row Brewing Co-Op hosts numerous events throughout the year, including an ugly Christmas sweater contest.

The Karen Wray Gallery

The Karen Wray Gallery, an independent art gallery located in Los Alamos, has represented more than 35 professional and emerging local artists since its opening in 2008. The gallery is just a short walk from the Bradbury Science Museum, and it's a popular place for visitors to peruse either before or after attending a program or event at the Bradbury. Local artists who currently have or have had their artwork on display at the gallery include Adam Baker, Sheridan Brown, Reva Heron, Cheryl Hoagland, Janice Parker Muir, Kim Mason, Anthony Ortiz, and Donato Spitzer. Artwork from these and other artists is available for purchase directly from the gallery or online. Exhibitions change every season, so visitors are sure to see new and exciting artwork no matter when they visit.

Best Time to Visit: The Karen Wray Gallery is open Monday through Friday from 11:00 a.m. to 4:00 p.m. and Saturday from 10:00 a.m. to 4:00 p.m.

Pass/Permit/Fees: There is no fee to visit the Karen Wray Gallery.

Closest City or Town: Los Alamos

Address: 1247 Central Avenue, Suite D-2, Los Alamos, NM 87544

GPS Coordinates: 35.88187° N, 106.29705° W

Did You Know? Aspiring artists can take classes at the Karen Wray Gallery, including oils classes, watercolor classes, and "Painting for the Absolute Beginner."

The Tsankawi Trail

Located in Bandelier National Monument, the Tsankawi Trail is a 1.5-mile hike along a volcanic mesa. Highlights of the hike include caves, petroglyphs, and the Ancestral Pueblo village of Tsankawi. This is an extremely difficult trek, as hikers are required to climb wooden ladders to reach the village, and the trail is open and exposed to the elements. Using the trail during thunderstorms or snowy weather is not advisable. There are also some narrow trenches and high spots, so this isn't a hike that's recommended for people who are claustrophobic or have a fear of heights. Once you reach the top of the mesa, though, the views are spectacular in all directions. The picturesque view of the Jemez Mountains and Los Alamos is particularly stunning. Hikers are sure to come across various native animals, including short-horned lizards.

Best Time to Visit: The best time to visit the trail is during the spring, summer, or fall when the weather is dry.

Pass/Permit/Fees: A 7-day pass to visit the Bandelier National Monument is $15, but there's no extra fee to visit the Tsankawi Trail.

Closest City or Town: Los Alamos

Address: Bandelier National Monument, 15 Entrance Road, Los Alamos, NM 87544

GPS Coordinates: 35.87196° N, 106.22412° W

Did You Know? At its peak, the Tsankawi Pueblo Village had approximately 300 rooms.

Upper Frijoles Falls

Near Bandelier National Monument, visitors can take an easy hike along Frijoles Creek to get to the Upper Frijoles Falls. The falls are 90 feet tall and just 1.4 miles from the trailhead. While you are hiking the Falls Trail, you'll come across Tent Rocks around volcanic vents, bushes, agaves, and deep canyons.

If you continue your hike past the falls, you'll come across ancient Anasazi dwellings that were carved into the landscape. You can also take a path that follows the Rio Grande through White Rock Canyon. On your hike, you may also encounter deer, snakes, and many colorful birds.

Best Time to Visit: The trails are open all year, but spring and summer are the most trafficked times due to the warm weather.

Pass/Permit/Fees: There is a $25 vehicle fee to access Bandelier National Monument.

Closest City or Town: Los Alamos

Address: Bandelier National Monument, 15 Entrance Road, Los Alamos, NM 87544

GPS Coordinates: 35.7634° N, 106.2597° W

Did You Know? If you are feeling particularly adventurous, you can hike to Cochiti Lake, which is about 14 miles from the falls. Along with Cochiti Lake, you'll be near the Cochiti pueblo.

Brazos Cliffs

The Brazos Cliffs reach roughly 3,000 feet into the sky at their highest point. While you can no longer climb the Brazos Cliffs because they are currently on private property, you can hike around the area and view its scenic beauty.

The best way to hike and view the cliffs is to get on the Tony Marques Trail (#41) in Carson National Forest. On this trail, you will experience stunning views of the cliffs as well as the Colorado border, Brazos Ridge Mountain Range, Sangre de Cristo Mountains, and more.

Best Time to Visit: Spring through fall offers the best weather for hiking.

Pass/Permit/Fees: The trails are free to hike.

Closest City or Town: Los Ojos

How to get there: Heron Lake State Park Visitor Center, 640 State Road 95, Los Ojos, NM 87551

GPS Coordinates: 36.7493° N, 106.3936° W

Did You Know? The rock that makes up the Brazos Cliffs is some of the oldest in the state of New Mexico. The Precambrian quartzite and plutonic rock date back 1.8 billion years. Additionally, the peak of the Brazos Cliffs is rounded, which also signifies its old age.

Heron Lake

For some of New Mexico's best fishing, camping, boating, hiking, and birdwatching, you must visit Heron Lake State Park in Rio Arriba County. For water sports, Heron Lake is perfect for kayaking, paddle boarding, and fishing because boats are not allowed to create a wake. Additionally, there are many hiking and cross-country skiing trails around the lake. Heron Lake sits among tall pine trees and offers views of the mountainous landscape. There is even a 5.5-mile trail that crosses a large suspension bridge and leads to nearby El Vado Lake.

Best Time to Visit: For water activities, the best time to visit is during the summer. However, you can trek the trails year-round.

Pass/Permit/Fees: There is a $5 entrance fee per vehicle. Camping and other activities may require additional fees.

Closest City or Town: Los Ojos

Address: Heron Lake Campground, 640 State Road 95, Los Ojos, NM 87551

GPS Coordinates: 36.6887° N, 106.6940° W

Did You Know? Visitors have reported some amazing wildlife around the area, such as mountain lions, black bears, elk, deer, marmots, bald eagles, osprey, and more. Regardless of whether you stay for a day or the entire week, you're bound to see some elusive animals and breathtaking views.

Casa Rondena Winery

Established in 1995, Casa Rodena Winery is a family endeavor. The first plantings took place in 1990, overseen by vintner John Calvin and his sons, Ross and Clayton. In 1997, the family opened the tasting room, and the winery building, complete with a commemorative tricentennial bell tower, was opened in 2004. The most recent addition to the winery is a new barrel-aging and storage facility designed to expand production, which was completed in 2008. In 2010, John Calvin's former home on the property was turned into the 1629 Club, a private club that requires a certain level of membership. Calvin is considered a pioneer of premium winemaking in New Mexico and has increased the public's knowledge of high-desert wines, including his signature Meritage Red, a Bordeaux-style blend of Cabernet Franc, Cabernet Sauvignon, and Merlot.

Best Time to Visit: The tasting room is open daily from 12:00 p.m. to 7:00 p.m.

Pass/Permit/Fees: There is no fee to visit the winery.

Closest City or Town: Albuquerque

Address: 733 Chavez Road NW, Los Ranchos de Albuquerque, NM 87107

GPS Coordinates: 35.15493° N, 106.64747° W

Did You Know? From 2011 to 2017, *Albuquerque* magazine readers named John Calvin the best vintner and Casa Rodena the best winery.

Turquoise Trail

The Turquoise Trail National Scenic Byway is a 15,000-square-mile historic and scenic area that connects Albuquerque and Santa Fe. As you drive the 50 miles of Highway 14, you'll travel through old mining towns and miles of gorgeous landscape, and there will be many opportunities to get out of the car and explore the trails. Don't forget to bring your camera because you'll have the chance to capture some of New Mexico's most famous scenic views at Tijeras, Cedar Crest, Sandia Park, and Cibola National Forest.

Best Time to Visit: You can drive along the road year-round but watch for severe weather because you don't want to get caught in a storm. Try driving at sunrise or sunset for the most breathtaking views.

Pass/Permit/Fees: There are no fees required to drive along the scenic byway.

Closest City or Town: Madrid

Address: Cerrillos Hills State Park, 37 Main Street, Los Cerrillos, NM 87010

GPS Coordinates: 35° 24' 21.00" N, 106° 09' 16.19" W

Did You Know? There are many places to stop and camp along the scenic byway, as well as numerous old mining towns that boast local art, crafts, theater, music, museums, and restaurants. Check out the local events in Golden, Madrid, and Cerrillos because they host many parades and festivals throughout the year.

North Fork Casa Falls

At 50 feet in height, North Fork Casa Falls makes up part of a 1,500-foot series of cascading waterfalls. Found in the Pecos Wilderness of Carson National Forest, Casa Falls is the most popular of the waterfalls in this area. There are others that you can visit if you are feeling adventurous. You can hike to North Fork Casa Falls fairly easily and see an abundance of wildlife along the way. Additionally, there won't be many people on the trails, so you can enjoy nature uninterrupted.

Best Time to Visit: May through October is the best time to visit the falls when the water and its flow are ideal.

Pass/Permit/Fees: There is no fee to visit the falls.

Closest City or Town: Mora

Address: Mora Visitor Center, NM-434, Mora, NM 87732

GPS Coordinates: 36°00.812° N, 105°28.903° W

Did You Know? If you are traveling to the falls and happen to get lost on your way, call Taos Search and Rescue. In 2018, an older couple got lost while they were trying to find the falls. The trail can be tricky to locate at some spots, so make sure you bring extra food and water just in case. Luckily, the 60-year-old couple had packed more than enough food, water, and emergency blankets to get them through the night. They were found unharmed by the rescue team.

Pecos National Historical Park

Pecos National Historical Park is often referred to as the "Gateway to the Plains," as it encompasses the woodlands of the Sangre de Cristo Mountains, the remains of Native American pueblos, and several geographic features that have played meaningful roles in the area's history. There is a pueblo, mission, Santa Fe Trail stage stop, and the sites of the westernmost Civil War battles. You'll also find Route 66 history and the summer home of Buddy Fogelson, a Texas oil magnate, and his wife, actress Greer Garson. The visitor center features an introductory film and a regional history and archeology museum.

Best Time to Visit: The best time to visit Pecos National Historical Park is in the spring, summer, or fall when the weather is warmer. It is open daily from 8:00 a.m. to 4:30 p.m.

Pass/Permit/Fees: There is no fee to visit Pecos National Historical Park.

Closest City or Town: Pecos

Address: 1 Peach Drive, Pecos, NM 87552

GPS Coordinates: 35.54993° N, 105.68853° W

Did You Know? The Glorieta Pass has served as a path through the Sangre de Cristo Mountains for thousands of years. Pueblo Indians, Plains Indians, Spanish conquerors, Spanish missionaries, Mexican armies, Santa Fe Trail settlers, and others all relied on this pass.

Red River Ski and Summer Area

The Red River Ski and Summer Area is a great ski resort that has snowshoeing and cross-country ski trails in the winter. There are many activities to do in the summer as well, such as hiking, backpacking, and horseback riding. You can also go ziplining and partake in numerous other family-friendly activities offered by the resort. When you are on the trails, you will see breathtaking views of the Sangre de Cristo Mountains and the southern part of the Rocky Mountains.

In the 19th century, the Red River was known as River City and favored by explorers, fur traders, and prospectors. The mountains were heavy with gold, silver, and copper mines, so many people traveled far and wide to settle in the area. The town of River City had its own red-light district, a dozen saloons, a dancing hall, and boarding houses.

Best Time to Visit: Because there are plenty of things to do, you can go during the winter months to ski and during the summer for other family-friendly activities.

Pass/Permit/Fees: Lift tickets cost up to $90 for skiing, and summer activity passes are generally around $25 per person. Otherwise, hiking is free for all.

Closest City or Town: Red River

Address: 400 Pioneer Road, Red River, NM 87558

GPS Coordinates: 36.7062° N, 105.4129° W

Did You Know? Red River was once home to the Ute and Jicarilla Apache tribes.

A Park Above

As the first fully inclusive and accessible playground in the state of New Mexico, A Park Above is a popular attraction for children of all ages and abilities. It is located on 6 acres of land and provides a place where children can play, interact, and grow, all while enjoying equipment at the park. Amenities include activity spaces with fencing and sensory surfacing, accessible playground equipment, a sport and basketball area, a splash pad, a hill with an ADA-compliant ramp, shade structures, outdoor musical instruments, adaptive swings, wheelchair swings, an amphitheater, a dog park, a bocce court, a labyrinth walking path, outdoor exercise equipment, a lawn area, and picnic tables. The wheelchair swings must be operated by trained staff who are not always present at the park.

Best Time to Visit: The best time to visit A Park Above is during the summer when the splash pad is open so that all amenities are available for use.

Pass/Permit/Fees: There is no fee to visit A Park Above.

Closest City or Town: Rio Rancho

Address: 3200 Civic Center Circle NE, Rio Rancho, NM 87144

GPS Coordinates: 35.22125° N, 106.68569° W

Did You Know? In 2014, about 35 volunteers planted 60 evergreen trees at A Park Above to reduce the impact of wind and blowing sand.

Rio Rancho Aquatic Center

Whether you want to swim laps, spend some pool time with your family, or need swimming lessons, the Rio Rancho Aquatic Center has got you covered. With three separate pools all designed for various purposes, visitors can exercise in the Cabezon Pool by swimming laps in one of the eight 25-yard lanes, play with their younger children in the zero-depth Rainbow Pool, or spend time with older kids in the Haynes Pool playing water basketball, water polo, or enjoying the water slides. The Rio Rancho Aquatic Center opened to the public in 2008 to provide a recreation and competition facility for the community and the public school system.

Best Time to Visit: The recreational pools are only open on Saturdays from 12:00 p.m. to 6:00 p.m. Lap swim is open for adults on Monday, Wednesday, and Thursday from 6:00 a.m. to 11:00 a.m. and again from 2:00 p.m. to 8:00 p.m. It's also available on Tuesdays from 2:00 p.m. to 8:00 p.m.

Pass/Permit/Fees: Admission is $4 for adults and $3 for children between the ages of 2 and 12. Children ages one and under are free.

Closest City or Town: Rio Rancho

Address: 745 Loma Colorado Drive NE, Rio Rancho, NM 87124

GPS Coordinates: 35.26950° N, 106.66342° W

Did You Know? The Rio Rancho Aquatic Center is the number-one-rated pool in Rio Rancho, according to Yelp.

The J & R Vintage Auto Museum and Bookstore

For automobile lovers, the J & R Vintage Auto Museum and Bookstore is a true gem. With more than 60 vintage cars and trucks on display, visitors can take a trip through history just by viewing these incredible automobiles. Each vehicle has a story behind it, including an authentic 1918 Model T, a 1912 Buick, and a 1969 Mercury Cougar that was once driven by one of the museum owners in high school. Along with the vehicles, guests will be fascinated by the memorabilia and timeless Americana that surround the cars and trucks. There are die-cast model collections, car restoration books, and much more. Most of the vehicles in the museum have been lovingly restored by the owners, Gab and Evonna Joiner.

Best Time to Visit: The J & R Vintage Auto Museum and Bookstore is open daily from 10:00 a.m. to 5:00 p.m.

Pass/Permit/Fees: Admission is $6 for adults, $3 for children between the ages of 6 and 12, and $5 for seniors. Children ages five and under are free.

Closest City or Town: Rio Rancho

Address: 3650 State Highway 528 NE, Rio Rancho, NM 87144

GPS Coordinates: 35.32375° N, 106.57163° W

Did You Know? Visitors may catch owner Gab Joiner in his restoration shop on site.

Willow Creek Trail

At nearly 1 mile in length, Willow Creek Trail is a packed-dirt loop trail located in Willow Creek Bosque, a 3.1-acre park that is ideal for birdwatching and wildlife viewing. There are several viewing locations along the trail, which are rated easy and ADA accessible. The bosque and trail are dog friendly, but dogs must remain on a leash. There is a dog-waste station available, so please pick up after your pets. The relatively flat trail takes visitors along the Rio Grande for a chance to spot owls, geese, cranes, and up to 175 different species in the bosque. Walk amongst the cottonwood trees and take some time to enjoy the scenic views of the Rio Grande. Wooden benches are placed throughout the park for resting or wildlife viewing.

Best Time to Visit: The best time to visit Willow Creek Trail is during the spring, summer, or fall when the weather is warmer.

Pass/Permit/Fees: There is no fee to visit Willow Creek Trail.

Closest City or Town: Rio Rancho

Address: Visit Rio Rancho, 3200 Civic Center Circle NE, Rio Rancho, NM 87144

GPS Coordinates: 35.30411° N, 106.57849° W

Did You Know? There's a second trail in Willow Creek Bosque that's a little longer than Willow Creek Trail. The North Loop Trail is 1.72 miles, but it's just as flat and easy as Willow Creek Trail.

Anderson Museum of Contemporary Art

The Anderson Museum of Contemporary Art, or AMoCA, was established in 1994 as a venue for showcasing artwork produced by former fellows of the Roswell Artist-in-Residence Program. As of today, there are more than 500 diverse art pieces in AMoCA's 12 galleries. Its 22,000 square feet of exhibition space has become the premier source of knowledge about contemporary art in the Roswell area. The collection is a diverse pool of paintings, prints, photographs, drawings, and sculptures that offers a glimpse of the ever-changing issues in art since the Roswell Artist-in-Residence Program was established in 1967. Visitors will be treated to all types of art, from figurative to non-objective, that represent the diversity of participating artists.

Best Time to Visit: The Anderson Museum of Contemporary Art is open Monday through Friday from 9:00 a.m. to 4:00 p.m. and Saturday and Sunday from 1:00 p.m. to 5:00 p.m.

Pass/Permit/Fees: There is no fee to visit the Anderson Museum of Contemporary Art.

Closest City or Town: Roswell

Address: 409 E. College Boulevard, Roswell, NM 88201

GPS Coordinates: 33.40956° N, 104.51691° W

Did You Know? The Roswell Artist-in-Residence Program was established by local businessman and artist Donald B. Anderson.

Bottomless Lakes State Park

Located near Roswell, Bottomless Lakes State Park is a popular recreation area for non-motorized boating, camping, fishing, swimming, hiking, birdwatching, and even scuba diving. The lakes at this park are actually water-filled sinkholes that range from 17 feet to 90 feet deep. They are a blue-green color, which is created from aquatic plants, and have the illusion of great depth even when they are on the shallower end. Other amenities at the park include a beach, playground, sand volleyball court, a group shelter, 24 individual picnic shelters, the historic Lea Lake Pavilion, ten developed campsites (32 total campsites), a visitor center, and wildlife-viewing blinds.

Best Time to Visit: The best time to visit Bottomless Lakes State Park is during the summer, when you can rent equipment for water activities and enjoy the warm weather.

Pass/Permit/Fees: There is no fee to visit Bottomless Lakes State Park unless you are camping. Camps range between $8 and $18 per night, depending on the site.

Closest City or Town: Roswell

Address: 545 A Bottomless Lakes Road, Roswell, NM 88201

GPS Coordinates: 33.34691° N, 104.33848° W

Did You Know? There are more than 4.5 miles of hiking and mountain-biking trails at Bottomless Lakes State Park, the longest being the Skidmarks Mountain Bike Trail at 3.3 miles in length.

General Douglas L. McBride Military Museum

Initially called the Luna Natatorium in 1918, the General Douglas L. McBride Military Museum opened to the public in 1985. The museum displays a blend of the historical and cultural heritage of the New Mexico Military Institute (NMMI) and its Corps of Cadets. It features numerous exhibits detailing cadet life, institute history, and military history (both U.S. and worldwide). The building that houses the museum is actually a dual-use structure that includes the New Mexico Military Institute's Enrollment and Development Center. To honor the building's original namesake, Lieutenant Antonio J. Luna, a graduate of the institute, the first floor of the building was renamed Luna Hall in 2009 and houses various offices for the NMMI. The museum is located on the second floor and focuses its 12 exhibit spaces on various historical aspects of the institute.

Best Time to Visit: The General Douglas L. McBride Military Museum is open Monday through Friday from 8:00 a.m. to 4:00 p.m.

Pass/Permit/Fees: There is no fee to visit the General Douglas L. McBride Military Museum.

Closest City or Town: Roswell

Address: 101 W. College Boulevard, Roswell, NM 88201

GPS Coordinates: 33.41188° N, 104.52556° W

Did You Know? Luna Natatorium once housed the first indoor swimming pool west of the Mississippi River.

85

Historical Center for Southeast New Mexico

This museum was established to gather, preserve, and interpret the history of Southeast New Mexico. It's housed in the former home of Mr. and Mrs. James Phelps White, which was built in 1912, the same year that New Mexico gained statehood. The house is filled with antiques, rare and historical books, over 14,000 photographs, hundreds of manuscripts, maps, obituaries, audio tapes, newspapers, and more. Additionally, the Community Room, located in the Archive Building, can be rented out for dinners, banquets, receptions, meetings, weddings, and parties. It has a capacity of 105 people (85 if seated). The center serves as a reminder of early 20th-century life in Chaves County, New Mexico.

Best Time to Visit: The Historical Center for Southeast New Mexico is open only by appointment. Call 575-622-8333 to book a visit.

Pass/Permit/Fees: There is no fee to visit the Historical Center for Southeast New Mexico.

Closest City or Town: Roswell

Address: 200 N. Lea Avenue, Roswell, NM 88201

GPS Coordinates: 33.39530° N, 104.52922° W

Did You Know? The house is styled in the Prairie, or Schooner, design that Frank Lloyd Wright developed in the early 1900s.

International UFO Museum and Research Center

In 1947, an unidentified flying object (UFO) crash-landed on a ranch near Roswell. Debris from the crash was later found by rancher W. W. "Mack" Brazel, who said he was struck by the unusual debris material. Other ranchers told him he might have found the wreckage of an alien spacecraft or a government project. Eventually, the Army Air Forces released a statement that a "flying disk had been found." However, subsequently, the U.S. government has backpedaled from these claims and stated that it was "nothing more than a weather balloon." Visitors to the International UFO Museum and Research Center can learn all about "The Roswell Incident" and make up their own minds about what really happened.

Best Time to Visit: The International UFO Museum and Research Center is open daily from 9:00 a.m. to 5:00 p.m.

Pass/Permit/Fees: Admission is $5 for adults, $2 for children between the ages of 5 and 15, and $3 for seniors, military personnel, and first responders.

Closest City or Town: Roswell

Address: 114 N. Main Street, Roswell, NM 88203

GPS Coordinates: 33.39440° N, 104.52296° W

Did You Know? Some witnesses say that there were alien bodies discovered with the wreckage, but the nurse who claimed to see them was transferred to England and was never heard from again.

Roswell

Roswell is a city in New Mexico that is situated at the convergence of the Spring, Hondo, and Pecos rivers. Originally home to the Mescalero Apaches and used as hunting grounds by Comanche tribes, Roswell was officially established by Van Smith in 1870.

Roswell is the site of numerous UFO sightings and unexplainable incidents, such as the time a farmer found unidentifiable debris in his sheep pasture that supposedly belonged to the government-based Project Mogul. Today, Roswell features many art pieces, history, and even the International UFO Museum and Research Center, which is home to The Alien Caffeine Espresso Bar.

Best Time to Visit: The best times to visit Roswell are late spring and the fall because the weather will be dry and mild. In the summer, temperatures get hot, and winters may be cooler.

Pass/Permit/Fees: There are no fees to enter Roswell, but you may have to pay to visit the museums.

Closest City or Town: Roswell

Address: Roswell Visitor Center, 426 N. Main Street, Roswell, NM 88201

GPS Coordinates: 33.3943° N, 104.5230° W

Did You Know? Roswell is the UFO capital of the world and will be hosting annual UFO festivals starting in 2021.

Roswell Historic District

With more than 200 independent shops, galleries, restaurants, businesses, and performing arts facilities, the Roswell Historic District has something that will appeal to everyone. Visit the Ann Jackson Gallery or the Synergy Fine Art Gallery to view artwork from local artists. Check out Mojo Vinyl Records to find that rare record from your favorite vintage band, or shop at Uniquities to discover that must-have décor item for your home. Don't forget to make a stop at Serendipity to buy a unique souvenir of your time in Roswell. When you get hungry, try Adele's on Canton, Diesel Pizza & Pub, or Ceviche Taqueria for some authentic Southwestern cuisine. Then, take a walk through the city to view the eclectic sculptures that makeup Art Around Roswell, or tour the two historic house museums of Barrington Hall and Bullock Hall.

Best Time to Visit: The best time to visit is during the spring, summer, or fall when the weather is ideal.

Pass/Permit/Fees: There is no fee to visit Roswell Historic District.

Closest City or Town: Roswell

Address: Roswell Visitor Center, 426 N. Main Street, Roswell, NM 88201

GPS Coordinates: 34.01444° N, 84.36521° W

Did You Know? The Roswell Historic District earned a spot on the National Register of Historic Places in 1985. It contains approximately 298 historic buildings, including the James Phelps White House.

Spring River Park and Zoo

This 34-acre park and zoo has five main zoo areas that work to enrich the lives of the Roswell community through exposure to native wildlife. Exhibits include *Capitan Trail, Around the World, Mountain Habitats, Ranch Heritage Exhibit,* and *Carousel and Train Rides. Capitan Trail* features small native animals like foxes and raccoons and larger animals like bison, aoudad, and deer. *Around the World* includes animals like lemurs, ravens, wallabies, beavers, and more. *Mountain Habitats* showcases the zoo's two black bears, a bobcat, and an aoudad, in their natural habitats. The *Ranch Heritage Exhibit* includes longhorns and miniature horses, and the *Carousel and Train Rides* area features an antique wooden-horse carousel and a miniature train from 1976.

Best Time to Visit: The Spring River Park and Zoo is open daily from 10:00 a.m. to 4:00 p.m.

Pass/Permit/Fees: Adult admission is $5 for Roswell residents and $10 for non-residents. Children ages 4 to 15 are $2.50 for Roswell residents and $3.50 for nonresidents.

Closest City or Town: Roswell

Address: 1306 E. College Boulevard, Roswell, NM 88201

GPS Coordinates: 33.40785° N, 104.50400° W

Did You Know? Although aoudads are originally native to North Africa, they adapted well to the climate in New Mexico and were introduced to the region after World War II.

90

Walker Aviation Museum

The Walker Aviation Museum is dedicated to displaying historical information about Roswell's military base and the men and women who served there. Roswell Army Air Field and Walker Air Force Base housed the Strategic Air Command's most elite fighting force. The location of Roswell's base was vital to the country's security. The Roswell Army Air Field was also home to the Roswell Army Flying School. The museum is temporarily located in the Roswell International Air Center Terminal as it awaits the funds to move to a permanent location. The Air Force base was officially closed on June 30, 1967, following 26 years of service, but the Walker Aviation Museum was established by Johnny Stites and his wife Maralea to display aviation artifacts and military aircraft models to honor the soldiers who were stationed at the base throughout its history.

Best Time to Visit: The Walker Aviation Museum is open daily from 10:00 a.m. to 3:30 p.m.

Pass/Permit/Fees: There is no fee to visit the Walker Aviation Museum.

Closest City or Town: Roswell

Address: 1 Jerry Smith Circle, Roswell, NM 88203

GPS Coordinates: 33.30751° N, 104.51935° W

Did You Know? The Walker Aviation Museum is named for General Kenneth Newton Walker, a New Mexico native who was killed in 1943 during a bombing mission over Papua New Guinea.

Ruidoso

Ruidoso is a small mountain town in the Sierra Blanca Mountains. First inhabited by the Mescalero Apache, the area was named Rio Ruidoso by Spanish settlers, which literally translates to "noisy river." The town itself is deeply rooted in Native American culture and offers horseback riding, hiking, camping, and rustic cabins for glamorous camping. Additionally, you can glide down one of the longest ziplines in the world, an 8,900-foot zipline at Ski Apache. There are also numerous casinos and performing arts centers.

Best Time to Visit: There are things to do at all times of the year. Visitors can hike or camp in the summer and ski or take sleigh rides when there is snow. For winter travel, Ruidoso visitor guides recommend four-wheel drive and chains in case of a storm. Generally, there is rain in the spring and fall, and April and May can get a bit windy.

Pass/Permit/Fees: There is no fee to enter Ruidoso, but you will need to pay for the attractions.

Closest City or Town: Ruidoso

Address: Ruidoso Visitor Center, 720 Sudderth Drive, Ruidoso, NM 88345

GPS Coordinates: 33.3673° N, 105.6588° W

Did You Know? When visiting Ruidoso, you can enjoy the many cultural and historical attractions, such as the counties where Billy the Kid roamed.

Three Rivers Waterslides

Contrary to its name, Three Rivers Waterslides is actually a small waterfall that flows over smooth rocks to form a natural water slide. If you do choose to slide, however, know that it will not be the same as a man-made one, and your backside may hurt afterward. The water slides are at about 7,900 feet of elevation and can be found in the Lincoln National Forest.

The Three Rivers Waterslides waterfall is part of the 11 miles of trail known as the Three Rivers Trail. Once you have been on the trail for about 3 miles, you will see the waterfalls on the right side.

Best Time to Visit: The best time to visit Three Rivers Waterslides is from May to October because these will be the warmest months. You can hike in the area in the winter, but you will likely need snowshoes, and you won't be able to slide down the rock. The trail is difficult, so bring enough water.

Pass/Permit/Fees: There are no fees to hike the trails in Lincoln National Forest.

Closest City or Town: Ruidoso

Address: Ruidoso Visitor Center, 720 Sudderth Drive, Ruidoso, NM 88345

GPS Coordinates: 33.40313° N, 105.8548° W

Did You Know? The Three Rivers Trail is rated as difficult because of the length and the total 3,444 feet of elevation that you will traverse along the way.

Bosque del Apache National Wildlife Refuge

Established in 1939, the Bosque del Apache National Wildlife Refuge features numerous trails, guided tours, fishing, and more within the 57,331 acres of park. You can choose to hike on the Desert Arboretum, Observation Blind Trail, Boardwalk Trail, Sparrow Loop, John P. Taylor Jr. Memorial Trail, Bajada Loop, Marsh Overlook Trail, and more to see unique wildlife and gorgeous scenery. You'll see reptiles, birds, mammals, and more while exploring. Plus, the wildlife that frequents the park is often seasonal, so you'll see different animals depending on when you visit.

Best Time to Visit: The park is open year-round, and visitors can enter between sunrise and sunset.

Pass/Permit/Fees: There is a $5 entrance fee per vehicle.

Closest City or Town: San Antonio

Address: 1001 NM-1, San Antonio, NM 87832

GPS Coordinates: 33.8045° N, 106.8911° W

Did You Know? The Sandhill Crane (*Grus Canadensis*) is a frequent resident of the wildlife refuge. This crane is present in the park from late October to about mid-February. They have roughly ten different calls and do elaborate dances for courtship. If you are interested in birdwatching, consider visiting the park when these cranes are present.

Tinkertown Museum

Founded by Ross Ward, a painter, carver, and tinker, Tinkertown Museum is home to a massive collection of miniatures, memorabilia, Americana, and other eccentric collections. You'll find more than 50,000 glass bottles that were used to form the walls of the 22-room museum, along with a miniature Western town that comes to life in front of your eyes. There's a tiny circus, complete with miniature tigers, high-wire performers, and even a mini Fat Lady. Don't forget to have your fortune told by Esmerelda, the Fortune Teller, by feeding her machine a quarter and stop to listen to Otto, the one-man band, as you gaze upon antique tools, bullet pencils, and more. Among all the tiny wood-carved figures that were lovingly created by Ward himself, there's a surprisingly large antique wooden sailboat that once completed a 10-year trip around the world.

Best Time to Visit: Tinkertown Museum is open April through September, Friday through Monday, from 10:00 a.m. and 4:00 p.m. The last tickets are sold at 3:30 p.m.

Pass/Permit/Fees: Adult admission is $6 per person, and children between the ages of 4 and 16 are $3 per person. Children ages three and under are free.

Closest City or Town: Sandia Park

Address: 121 Sandia Crest Road, Sandia Park, NM 87047

GPS Coordinates: 35.17032° N, 106.36737° W

Did You Know? Tinkertown Museum entertains more than 20,000 visitors each year.

Canyon Road

Along the half-mile Canyon Road in Santa Fe, visitors can discover more than 100 restaurants, boutiques, and galleries that are dedicated to promoting fine art from artists across the world. The galleries that line Canyon Road feature all styles of art. You can add to your collection or simply view incredible works from established or emerging artists.

Canyon Road galleries often have strong positive reputations with major art museums, collectors, and art fairs throughout the country. Interspersed among the galleries are some of Santa Fe's finest jewelry stores and top restaurants, making a trip to Canyon Road a full experience.

Best Time to Visit: The best time to visit Canyon Road is during the Spring Art Festival (held in May) or the Historic Canyon Road Paint and Sculpt Out (held in October).

Pass/Permit/Fees: There is no fee to visit Canyon Road.

Closest City or Town: Santa Fe

Address: Santa Fe Visitor Center, 491 Old Santa Fe Trail, Santa Fe, NM 87505

GPS Coordinates: 35.68281° N, 105.92849° W

Did You Know? Originally, Canyon Road was a trail that led from the Ogha Po-oge pueblo (where modern-day Santa Fe is located) to the mountains.

Camel Rock

To see one of New Mexico's most unique rock structures, head to Camel Rock. Camel Rock is exactly what it sounds like: a rock that resembles the shape of a camel. You can easily see this sitting camel from U.S. Highway 285. If you take the exit, you will find a parking area and walking path to the 40-foot-tall, 100-foot-long rock structure. The sandstone is a light pink and tan color, which adds to the structure's camel-like appearance.

Best Time to Visit: You can visit Camel Rock year-round. However, the spring and summer will likely have more visitors.

Pass/Permit/Fees: No fees are required to visit Camel Rock.

Closest City or Town: Santa Fe

Address: 385 Frontage, Camel Rock, Santa Fe, NM 87506

GPS Coordinates: 35.7695° N, 105.9472° W

Did You Know? In late January or early February of 2017, the camel's nose came loose and fell off the rock structure. However, the difference is so minute that most visitors won't be able to notice that the camel looks any different.

Cathedral Basilica of St. Francis of Assisi

The original Cathedral of Santa Fe was built in 1610, but this building was replaced by a larger facility in 1630 and then destroyed by the Pueblo Indian Revolt of 1680. There is still a small part of this church in existence today in the form of the small adobe chapel that has been dedicated to *Our Lady La Conquistadora*. The statue was brought from Spain to Santa Fe in 1625, and it's the oldest representation of the Virgin Mary in the country. A new cathedral was ordered in 1850 and completed in 1887. Due to a lack of funds, the cathedral's spires were never completed. Structural reinforcement was added in 1967, along with new sacristies. In 2005, Pope Benedict XVI elevated the cathedral to a basilica, which means it holds particular importance in Rome and internationally.

Best Time to Visit: The best time to visit the Cathedral Basilica of St. Francis of Assisi is during Mass, which is held Monday through Friday at 12:10 p.m., Saturday at 4:00 p.m., and Sunday at 8:00 a.m., 9:00 a.m., and 11:00 a.m.

Pass/Permit/Fees: There is no fee to visit the Cathedral Basilica of St. Francis of Assisi.

Closest City or Town: Santa Fe

Address: 131 Cathedral Place, Santa Fe, NM 87501

GPS Coordinates: 35.68747° N, 105.93622° W

Did You Know? Seven archbishops, including Father John Baptiste Lamy, are buried in the cathedral's sanctuary.

El Rancho de Las Golondrinas

Translated as "The Ranch of the Swallows," El Rancho de Las Golondrinas is a historic ranch that has been transformed into a living history museum. Its origins trace back to the early 1700s when the ranch was an important stop along the Camino Real, or the Royal Road, between Mexico City, Mexico, and Santa Fe. The ranch offered various goods for trade and even hosted the famous colonial military leader and governor Don Juan Bautista de Anza in 1780. Various festivals are held at the ranch throughout the year, including the Santa Fe Spring & Fiber Fest, the Harvest Festival, the Santa Fe Herb & Lavender Festival, and the Santa Fe Spirits of New Mexico Halloween Event. The ranch is 200 acres in size and preserves the time period when Spain ruled in the New Mexico area in the 18th and 19th centuries.

Best Time to Visit: The best time to visit El Rancho de Las Golondrinas is when there's a festival.

Pass/Permit/Fees: The fee to visit El Rancho de Las Golondrinas depends on the fee for the festival you're attending. If you're not visiting during a festival, then it's free.

Closest City or Town: Santa Fe

Address: 334 Los Pinos Road, Santa Fe, NM 87507

GPS Coordinates: 35.57508° N, 106.11139° W

Did You Know? El Rancho de Las Golondrinas opened as a museum in 1972 to preserve and celebrate the history and culture of the Santa Fe area.

Georgia O'Keeffe Museum

This museum celebrates the life of one of the most significant 20th-century artists: Georgia O'Keeffe. It opened in 1997, over a decade after O'Keeffe passed away. The museum highlights her paintings and creative process alongside two of her homes and studios, a research center, and a library. O'Keeffe was dedicated to painting what she called "the wideness and wonder of the world as I live in it." Her artwork is instantly recognizable by her abstractions and large-scale depictions of natural objects, cityscapes, and unusual shapes that represent the landscape and architecture of northern New Mexico.

Best Time to Visit: The Georgia O'Keeffe Museum is open Monday, Thursday, Friday, Saturday, and Sunday from 10:00 a.m. to 5:00 p.m.

Pass/Permit/Fees: General admission is $20 for adults ages 18 and up. Children under the age of 18 are free.

Closest City or Town: Santa Fe

Address: 217 Johnson Street, Santa Fe, NM 87501

GPS Coordinates: 35.68931° N, 105.94128° W

Did You Know? The Georgia O'Keeffe Museum houses a collection of 3,000 works by O'Keeffe, ranging from oil paintings to drawings. Hundreds of works date between 1904 and her final year of work in 1984 when failing eyesight forced her into retirement. The museum rotates the selection of works on display, so every visit is unique.

100

Jemez Falls

Located in the Santa Fe National Forest, Jemez Falls is 70 feet high and generally has a healthy flow of water. These are the highest falls in the Jemez Mountains and are an easy quarter-mile hike from the paved parking lot. The trail ends at an overlook of the falls, and visitors should expect to spend about 45 minutes completing the loop. While you can easily get to the overlook from the parking lot, some visitors opt to use East Fork Trail (4 miles round trip) for a more rigorous hike.

Archeological findings in the Jemez Canyon and Soda Dam indicate that humans have been migrating through the area for thousands of years. Eventually, pueblos were formed, and as many as 30,000 people called the valley home.

Best Time to Visit: The best time to visit Jemez Falls is during the summer, but this is also when the trail is at its busiest.

Pass/Permit/Fees: There are no fees required to use the trails.

Closest City or Town: Jemez Springs

How to get there: Santa Fe National Forest Headquarters, 11 Forest Lane, Santa Fe, NM 87508

GPS Coordinates: 35.8125° N, 106.6069° W

Did You Know? Evidence of human life in the Jemez Valley dates back as far as 2500 BCE.

Loretto Chapel

Loretto Chapel was first conceived in 1850 when Bishop Jean Baptiste Lamy wanted to build a place to teach girls in the New Mexico Territory. The school was completed in 1853, and in 1873, the sisters began construction on the chapel. But when the Loretto Chapel was completed in 1878, there wasn't a way to get up to the choir loft 22 feet above the floor. Local carpenters said the only way to reach it would be by ladder because a staircase would reduce seating space inside the small chapel. Legend has it that after the sisters prayed to St. Joseph, an unknown man appeared with a hammer and square looking for work. He built the Miraculous Staircase with wood that was not native to the area and then disappeared without pay. Some believe the man was St. Joseph himself. The staircase design was so complex that experts today are baffled by how someone could have built the stairs with only wooden pegs.

Best Time to Visit: The chapel is open every day except Christmas Day from 9:00 a.m. to 5:00 a.m. Check the website calendar for private-event closures.

Pass/Permit/Fees: There is no fee to visit Loretto Chapel.

Closest City or Town: Santa Fe

Address: 207 Old Santa Fe Trail, Santa Fe, NM 87501

GPS Coordinates: 35.68601° N, 105.93751° W

Did You Know? The Miraculous Staircase at the Loretto Chapel has two full 360-degree turns with no structural support pole in the center.

Meow Wolf

This one-of-a-kind museum/amusement park is home to immersive and interactive exhibits that provide visitors with colorful, fantastical, and whimsical experiences. Meow Wolf opened in 2008 thanks to an informal group of artists in Santa Fe. The group consisted of graphic designers, musicians, writers, fabricators, painters, sculptors, and other artists who wanted to create "immersive maximalist environments that encourage audience participation." The main attraction at Meow Wolf is a combination jungle gym, mystery house, immersive art exhibit, and children's museum called The House of Eternal Return. With fluorescent colors under a blacklight and 20,000 square feet of room to explore, visitors can experience something new with every visit.

Best Time to Visit: Meow Wolf is open Monday and Thursday from 10:00 a.m. to 8:00 p.m., Friday and Saturday from 10:00 a.m. to 10:00 p.m., and Sunday from 9:00 a.m. to 8:00 p.m.

Pass/Permit/Fees: Admission is $35 for adults, $20 for children between the ages of 5 and 13, and $25 for seniors ages 65 and older.

Closest City or Town: Santa Fe

Address: 1352 Rufina Circle, Santa Fe, NM 87507

GPS Coordinates: 35.65540° N, 105.99700° W

Did You Know? Visitors are encouraged to explore the exhibits at their own pace and take as many pictures as possible.

Nambe Falls

Nambe Falls is a series of two waterfalls that are 75 feet and 100 feet tall. From the short trails, you can see the beautiful waterfalls as well as the Pueblo of Nambe, which manages the trails and the surrounding area of Nambe Falls. At the falls, there are opportunities to hike, swim, fish for cutthroat trout and salmon, picnic, and go camping. There are hiking trails below the falls and leading to an overlook, and all provide beautiful scenery.

Best Time to Visit: The mildest temperatures will be in the spring and fall, but visiting the falls in the summer may be better for water activities.

Pass/Permit/Fees: It costs $15 for admission to the falls.

Closest City or Town: Santa Fe

Address: 15A NP 102 West, Santa Fe, NM 87506

GPS Coordinates: 35.8456° N, 105.9064° W

Did You Know? Further downstream, you'll find a man-made dam. The United States government began construction on the Nambe Falls Dam in 1974 and completed it in 1976. About 300 miles upstream of Nambe Falls, the dam is a 150-foot-tall concrete structure that provides water for Pojoaque Valley Irrigation District and the pueblos of San Ildefonso, Nambe, and Pojoaque.

Ojo Caliente Mineral Springs

The healing power of water has been recognized by multiple cultures throughout the world. You can visit this 1,100-acre health resort for a relaxing experience, complete with a full-service spa that offers restorative therapy, massage, mud area, and other body treatments. Additionally, the Artesian Restaurant and Wine Bar features dishes with Ojo Caliente's own herbs, fruits, and vegetables.

Ojo Caliente Mineral Springs is one of the oldest natural wellness resorts in the United States. It opened its doors in 1868, but its waters have been thought to hold curative powers for thousands of years by Indigenous groups.

Best Time to Visit: Ojo Caliente is open year-round, so visitors can stop by whenever they are exploring the area. There are also camping and RV parks available that would be best to use in the spring and summer.

Pass/Permit/Fees: Treatments and amenities cost between $12 and $55, and entrance into Mineral Springs costs up to $38 per person.

Closest City or Town: Santa Fe

Address: 50 Los Banos Drive, Ojo Caliente, NM 87549

GPS Coordinates: 36.3043° N, 106.0524° W

Did You Know? Ojo Caliente is the only hot spring in the world that uses four distinct sulfur-free mineral waters.

Resumidero Falls

Resumidero Falls is comprised of three drops of 30 feet, 15 feet, and 20 feet. In total, Resumidero Falls is about 70 feet tall. One of the falls is truly unique in that it falls through a hole that has been naturally made in solid granite rock.

This is not an easy waterfall to reach, but Resumidero Falls is worth the trek. There is no distinct hiking path to the falls, but some have had success traveling from Vivian Falls, which is less than half a mile away. However, most people reach the falls by hiking south from the Rio Puerco campsite. If you don't start at the campsite, you can access the river from Forest Road 93.

Best Time to Visit: The best times to visit the area are in the summer and fall because the water from the falls is cold. The summers can get hot, so bring water.

Pass/Permit/Fees: No fees or reservations are required to visit the falls or the camping areas.

Closest City or Town: Santa Fe

Address: Santa Fe National Forest Headquarters, 11 Forest Lane, Santa Fe, NM 87508

GPS Coordinates: 36.114451° N, 106.746919° W

Did You Know? These falls are an absolute hidden treasure, and some visitors have reported seeing wild horses near them.

San Miguel Mission Chapel

The San Miguel Mission Chapel is the oldest Catholic church in the United States. It's located in Barrio de Analco, a national historic district in Santa Fe. Mexican Indians from Tlaxcala established the barrio prior to the 17th century, and an adobe church was constructed so that Franciscan friars could provide Catholic services to the small congregation of laborers, soldiers, and Indians who lived in Barrio de Analco at the time. This original structure was partially destroyed during the Pueblo Revolt of 1680, and the current chapel was built in 1710. The San Miguel Mission Chapel still has the original walls from the first structure and is regularly used for religious services.

Best Time to Visit: The best time to visit the San Miguel Mission Chapel is during meditation times, which are held Monday, Tuesday, Wednesday, and Friday from 1:00 p.m. to 3:00 p.m., Thursday from 11:00 a.m. to 3:00 p.m., and Sunday from 3:00 p.m. to 5:00 p.m.

Pass/Permit/Fees: There is no fee to visit the San Miguel Mission Chapel.

Closest City or Town: Santa Fe

Address: 401 Old Santa Fe Trail, Santa Fe, NM 87501

GPS Coordinates: 35.68433° N, 105.93764° W

Did You Know? In 1859, Archbishop John Baptiste Lamy purchased the chapel and the adjacent land to build a Catholic school. This became St. Michael's High School. The school was relocated in 1968, but the original building still stands.

Santa Fe Opera House

Now in its 64th season, the Santa Fe Opera House is committed to advancing the "operatic form by presenting ensemble performances of the highest quality in a unique setting with a varied repertory of new, rarely performed, and standard works." Over a season that lasts less than two months, the Santa Fe Opera House hosts 30 performances of four operas. In 2021, the ensemble produced performances of *The Lord of Cries* by John Corigliano and Mark Adamo, *A Midsummer Night's Dream, The Marriage of Figaro,* and *Eugene Onegin.* The opera house has been hosting performances since 1957 and continues to strive to expand opera's reach to diverse audiences. Since its opening, it has hosted 2,000 performances of 175 operas representing 89 composers.

Best Time to Visit: The best time to visit the opera house is from July 1 to the end of August.

Pass/Permit/Fees: The fee to visit the Santa Fe Opera House depends on seat and show selection. See the website for pricing details.

Closest City or Town: Santa Fe

Address: 301 Opera Drive, Santa Fe, NM 87506

GPS Coordinates: 35.76467° N, 105.94667° W

Did You Know? The Santa Fe Opera House sits on 199 acres of land formerly occupied by a guest ranch. It was established by New York-based conductor John Crosby. Its opening opera was Puccini's *Madama Butterfly.*

Blue Hole

Originally known as Blue Lake, Blue Hole is a geographical wonder that was created during a phenomenon known as the Santa Rosa Sink. The lake itself is one of seven lakes that are connected via an underground water system. Because it sits in the middle of an arid desert with little water around it, nomadic tribes, cowboys, and travelers alike visited this oasis.

Nowadays, visitors can swim, dive, and jump into Blue Hole on a hot summer's day. The visibility through Blue Hole's water is nearly 100 feet because the water is replaced on its own every 6 hours. The hole itself is 81 feet deep and has a diameter of 60 feet.

Best Time to Visit: The summer is the best time to visit because the water at Blue Hole is cold and will be refreshing in the heat.

Pass/Permit/Fees: The entrance fee is $20 per person.

Closest City or Town: Santa Rosa

Address: 1085 Blue Hole Road, Santa Rosa, NM 88435

GPS Coordinates: 34.9404° N, 104.6732° W

Did You Know? Even though the hole becomes a new lake four times a day, the temperature of the water always remains 62°F.

Holden Prong Cascades

The Holden Prong Cascades are unique gems when it comes to New Mexico's waterfalls. Situated in Gila National Forest, the Holden Prong Cascades are a series of waterfalls that are found along the 11-mile Holden Prong Trail No. 114. This trail features aspen and mixed conifer forests as well as many small pools and falls. Rated as an intermediate-level trail, you'll experience a 2,460-foot change in elevation and end at 8,700 feet above sea level. Visitors can hike, camp, horseback ride, and backpack along the trail to see its gorgeous views and beautiful landscape.

Best Time to Visit: Visitors should plan to hike the cascades during the spring and fall. Winter can have snow, which makes the trails difficult to travel.

Pass/Permit/Fees: No fees are required.

Closest City or Town: Silver City

Address: Gila National Forest, 3005 E. Camino del Bosque, Silver City, NM 88061

GPS Coordinates: 33.0123° N, 107.7440° W

Did You Know? There are numerous loops within Holden Prong that are up to 30 miles each, so there are many opportunities for backpacking and camping. The best camping in Holden Prong is a 2-mile area above the confluence of Water Canyon. If you try to camp in the upper section of Holden Prong, you'll run into forests that are too dense.

Gila Cliff Dwellings National Monument

While not as large as the Mesa Verde cliff dwellings in southern Colorado, the Gila cliff dwellings are just as impressive and enlightening. There are 46 rooms located in six caves that were carved into the cliff face in approximately 1300 CE by the Mogollon Native Americans. Before the Mogollon people decided to make the caves their permanent home, the Gila River caves were used by groups of nomadic Native Americans for temporary shelter. The Mogollon people stayed in their cliff dwellings for just 20 years but left behind their structures and pottery for modern society. Follow the moderately difficult 1-mile Cliff Dweller Trail to the dwellings to view these incredibly sturdy and well-preserved structures.

Best Time to Visit: The best time to visit the Gila Cliff Dwellings National Monument is during the spring, summer, or fall when the weather is dry.

Pass/Permit/Fees: The fee to visit the Gila Cliff Dwellings National Monument is $10 per person.

Closest City or Town: Silver City

Address: 26 Jim Bradford Trail, Mimbres, NM 88049

GPS Coordinates: 33.22779° N, 108.27232° W

Did You Know? Archeologists believe that between 10 and 15 families lived in the Gila cliff dwellings. It isn't currently known why the Mogollon people abandoned the site after two decades.

Very Large Array

The Very Large Array is a top astronomical radio observatory that consists of 28 radio antennas arranged in a Y-shaped configuration (which is how the facility got its name). Each antenna is 82 feet in diameter, and the data received by the antennas are electronically combined to create the equivalent of a 22-mile-diameter antenna. At any given time, 27 antennas are operational, and one is undergoing maintenance. Each antenna is mounted on double parallel railroad tracks so that the antenna sensitivity and angular resolution can be adjusted. Astronomers have made significant observations from the Very Large Array, including black holes and protoplanetary disks near young stars.

Best Time to Visit: The Very Large Array is open from 8:30 a.m. to sunset daily. Tours are available on the first and third Saturdays of the month at 11:00 a.m., 1:00 p.m., and 3:00 p.m.

Pass/Permit/Fees: Admission is $6 for adults and $5 for seniors ages 65 and older. Children ages 17 and under are free.

Closest City or Town: Socorro

How to get there: Socorro Heritage and Visitors Center, 217 Fisher Avenue, Socorro, NM 87801

GPS Coordinates: 34.07935° N, 107.61849° W

Did You Know? There is also a visitor center, museum, theater, and gift shop at the Very Large Array.

El Salto Falls

The El Salto del Agua Cañoncito Trail to reach El Salto Falls is just over 5 miles. The trail is an out-and-back hike that's generally lightly trafficked. However, the trail is rated as difficult because there is a 1,040-foot gain in elevation. In fact, it's so difficult that hikers must call the warden (505-398-0090) before coming to the trail. The falls are 200 feet tall at nearly 9,000 feet in elevation. El Salto Falls is composed of five separate drops that make for a beautiful and elaborate waterfall.

Best Time to Visit: The fall and spring are the best times to visit because the stream that makes up the falls is light and may dry up in the summer.

Pass/Permit/Fees: There is a $5 fee per person to hike this trail because it's on private land.

Closest City or Town: Taos

Address: Taos Visitor Center, 1139 Paseo Del Pueblo Sur, Taos, NM 87571

GPS Coordinates: 36.5326° N, 105.5378° W

Did You Know? The El Salto waterfall is located on private land with about 2,000 acres of wilderness. It was given to Antonio Martinez in 1716 or 1717. Today, the land is owned by the descendants of the Martinez family, who also manage it. All the fees that are paid to use the trail go towards maintaining the land.

Hacienda de los Martinez

As one of the few northern New Mexico–style "Great Houses" still standing in the American Southwest from the late Spanish Colonial period, Hacienda de los Martinez captures the prominent themes of the early 1800s. The house was built in 1804 and served as an important trade center for the Spanish Empire's northern boundary. It was initially occupied by Severino Martinez, his wife, and their six children, one of whom (Padre Antonio Martinez) would later battle the French Bishop Lamy to ensure that Hispanic culture remained a part of the Catholic Church in the New Mexico territory. The hacienda provides visitors with an inside look at the life of Mexican settlers in the 19th century.

Best Time to Visit: Hacienda de los Martinez is open Monday through Friday from 10:00 a.m. to 5:00 p.m. and Sunday from 12:00 p.m. to 5:00 p.m.

Pass/Permit/Fees: Admission is $8 for adults and $4 for children between the ages 5 and 16. Children under the age of 5 are free.

Closest City or Town: Taos

Address: 708 Hacienda Road, Taos, NM 87571

GPS Coordinates: 36.40183° N, 105.60793° W

Did You Know? The annual Taos Trade Fair is held at this destination to celebrate and re-enact Spanish colonial life, which featured trade among Spanish settlers, Native Americans, and mountain men.

114

Kit Carson Museum

The Kit Carson Museum is housed in a former home of the famous frontiersman, who lived in Taos from 1843 until his death in 1868. The house was acquired by the local Masonic fraternity, and the museum is operated by the Kit Carson Memorial Foundation to honor and celebrate his life. The modest single-story adobe house was built in 1825 and became Carson's home when he married Maria Josefa Jaramillo, the daughter of a prominent Taos family, in 1843. Carson purchased the house as a wedding gift for Jaramillo, his third wife. Seven of the couple's eight children were born and raised here. The rooms that are on display at the museum have been restored to the Spanish Colonial and Territorial styles that were popular during Carson's time.

Best Time to Visit: The Kit Carson Museum is open Tuesday through Saturday from 11:00 a.m. to 4:00 p.m.

Pass/Permit/Fees: Admission is $10 for adults and $8 for seniors ages 62 and older. A discounted rate of $7 is available for teens, students, and veterans. Taos County residents and children ages 12 and under are free.

Closest City or Town: Taos

Address: 113 Kit Carson Road, Taos, NM 87571

GPS Coordinates: 36.40756° N, 105.57273° W

Did You Know? The Kit Carson Museum opened to the public in 1949 after six ownership changes following Carson's death.

Taos Gorge/Rio Grande Gorge

The 800-foot-long Taos Gorge was carved by the Rio Grande. The rock is comprised of volcanic basalt and ash, making this an utterly unique sight. Visitors can hike the 6-mile-long Rio Grande Gorge Trail that dips into the gorge and covers an impressive 1,309 feet in elevation.

Best Time to Visit: The trails and bridge are available to visit year-round. However, the trail is closed for long-term construction as of January 2021, so make sure to check conditions before you go.

Pass/Permit/Fees: No fees are required to hike the trails or visit the gorge's bridge.

Closest City or Town: Taos

Address: 1139 Paseo Del Pueblo Sur, Taos, NM 87571

GPS Coordinates: 36.4762° N, 105.7330° W

Did You Know? The Gorge Bridge sits 650 feet above the Rio Grande and is the fifth-highest bridge in the United States. Originally called "the bridge to nowhere," the Rio Grande Gorge Bridge was dedicated in 1965 and is currently part of U.S. Route 64. If you can conquer your fear of heights and cross the bridge, you will experience spectacular views of the gorge and the landscape surrounding the Rio Grande.

Taos Pueblo

Taos Pueblo is a living Native American community that features multi-story adobe structures that have been standing and inhabited for more than 1,000 years. It is the only living Native American community that has received both a World Heritage Site and National Historic Landmark designation. In 1906, the United States took 48,000 acres of land from the Taos Pueblo Native Americans. It wasn't until 1970 that this land was restored to the Taos Pueblo, and their traditional culture was allowed to continue. The act that returned the land to its rightful owners set a precedent for other tribes and nations in the country that had also suffered similar injustices. Feast Days is an annual festival celebrated by the Taos Pueblo, and although it's open to the public, you have to be invited to a home to share a feast-day meal.

Best Time to Visit: The best time to visit Taos Pueblo is during Feast Days, which occurs in late September. Visiting hours are Monday through Saturday from 8:00 a.m. to 4:30 p.m. and Sunday from 8:30 a.m. to 4:30 p.m.

Pass/Permit/Fees: There is no fee to visit Taos Pueblo.

Closest City or Town: Taos

Address: 120 Veterans Highway, Taos, NM 87571

GPS Coordinates: 36.44230° N, 105.54651° W

Did You Know? When observing dances at Taos Pueblo, you should not applaud after a dance is over. They are not performances but rather part of a sacred ceremony. You should also refrain from asking about their significance.

Taos Ski Valley

In the 1800s, Taos Ski Valley was home to a small copper-mining town known as Twining. Nowadays, Taos Ski Valley is a popular ski resort, and there are about 34,000 people living in the surrounding county. The ski resort is known for Kachina Peak, a mountain that reaches 12,481 feet above sea level.

In the winter, you'll find diverse ski trails that range from beginner to intermediate. Additionally, there are well-groomed trails, glades, moguls, and bowls with some of the lightest powder in all of North America. In the summer, Taos Ski Valley offers hiking, biking, climbing, fishing, and a range of other activities.

Best Time to Visit: There are year-round activities at Taos Ski Valley, but if you're planning to ski, you'll want to go in the winter months. For warm-weather activities, visit during the spring and fall for the mildest temperatures.

Pass/Permit/Fees: Tickets for the ski village cost between $65 and $85 for non-lift tickets and $90 to $128 for peak lift tickets.

Closest City or Town: Taos

Address: 116 Sutton Place, Taos Ski Valley, NM 87525

GPS Coordinates: 36.5960° N, 105.4545° W

Did You Know? The Kachina lift goes the highest of any triple-chair lift in North America.

The Millicent Rogers Museum

Millicent Rogers, the granddaughter of Henry Huttleson Rogers, a founder of the Standard Oil Company, was a notable entertainer and fashionista. She eventually settled in Taos and established friendships among the Taos artists' colony. Millicent passed away at a young age and left a collection of art, jewelry, and weavings that are on display in the museum that now bears her name. The Millicent Rogers Museum was founded in 1956 by her son Paul Peralta-Ramos to celebrate her memory and highlight the Southwest arts and culture that she found so fascinating while she was alive. Peralta-Ramos's friendship with famed potter Maria Martinez led to the donation of the largest publicly held collection of Martinez artwork in the world.

Best Time to Visit: The Millicent Rogers Museum is open daily from 10:00 a.m. to 5:00 p.m., except November through March, when it is closed on Wednesdays.

Pass/Permit/Fees: The fee to visit the Millicent Rogers Museum is $10 per person. Children ages 12 and under are free.

Closest City or Town: Taos

Address: 1504 Millicent Rogers Road, El Prado, NM 87529

GPS Coordinates: 36.44518° N, 105.59350° W

Did You Know? The museum is located in a hacienda donated by the estate of Mr. and Mrs. Claude Anderson.

Wheeler Peak

Located in the Sangre De Cristo Mountains, Wheeler Peak is the highest point in New Mexico. Wheeler Peak is named after U.S. Army Major George M. Wheeler, who did a lot of the surveying of New Mexico in the 1870s. Wheeler Peak Summit Trail #67 in Carson National Forest leads to the top. The trail begins at 10,200 feet and ends at the summit at 13,161 feet. In the 2.2 miles that it takes to get to the top of Wheeler Peak (after the 4.1 miles traveled on Williams Lake Trailhead), visitors will experience many mountain switchbacks, and the trail will become narrow at some points. This hike is rated as intermediate to expert and may not be suitable for beginner hikers.

Best Time to Visit: The best times to visit are the late spring, early summer, and fall to avoid the worst of the storms and monsoon season. Late May through November should be fine but plan your trip in the morning to avoid afternoon storms.

Pass/Permit/Fees: No fees are required to use the hiking trail.

Closest City or Town: Taos

Address: Taos Ski Valley, 116 Sutton Place, Taos Ski Valley, NM 87525

GPS Coordinates: 36.5569° N, 105.4168° W

Did You Know? No one knows who made the first complete climb of Wheeler Peak, but it was most likely the Taos Pueblo tribes who have historically inhabited the land.

Williams Falls

The trail leading to Williams Falls offers opportunities to hike, snowshoe, cross-country ski, or travel by horseback. Williams Falls is located near Williams Lake and Wheeler Peak, so you will have amazing views as you hike along the trail to this 35-foot-tall waterfall.

To access the waterfall, you simply hike down Williams Lake Trail in Carson National Forest. The lake is at an elevation of over 11,000 feet, which makes it quite a unique sight for anyone hiking through the mountains. You'll see amazing views of the mountains, towering trees, and an abundance of wildlife.

Best Time to Visit: This trail system can be accessed at all times of the year. For hiking or horseback riding, use the trail system during the summer; for cross-country skiing and snowshoeing, visit the trail during the winter months.

Pass/Permit/Fees: There are no fees to hike the trails in Carson National Forest.

Closest City or Town: Taos

Address: Taos Ski Valley, 116 Sutton Place, Taos Ski Valley, NM 87525

GPS Coordinates: 43.4880° N, 96.7692° W

Did You Know? Williams Lake is a natural lake, but it doesn't have any fish in its waters because it freezes completely during the winter.

White Rock Overlook Park Waterfall

White Rock Overlook Park is located near White Rock and Los Alamos. The waterfall on the White Rock Trail is part of a 7.8-mile trail system. It's a small, 7-foot dual waterfall that seemingly pops out of nowhere when you are on the trail. To get to the waterfalls, you will take the Red Dot or Blue Dot Trail and go through White Rock Canyon along the Rio Grande River. You'll also see petroglyphs, springs, and an abundance of wildlife.

Best Time to Visit: The spring or fall will have the mildest weather, but you can hike the trail in the summer. The summer will get hot, however, so bring plenty of water as there is not much shade.

Pass/Permit/Fees: There are no fees to park or hike the trails.

Closest City or Town: White Rock

Address: 700 Overlook Road, White Rock, NM 87547

GPS Coordinates: 35.48143° N, 106.11722° W

Did You Know? The trail is called the Red Dot (or Blue Dot) Trail because there are spray-painted dots that line the trail. These red dots make sure hikers don't get lost along the way because the trail can be hard to follow at times. If you're traveling to White Rock Overlook or the waterfalls, follow the red or blue dots.

Proper Planning

With this guide, you are well on your way to properly planning a marvelous adventure. When you plan your travels, you should become familiar with the area, save any maps to your phone for access without internet, and bring plenty of water—especially during the summer months. Depending on which adventure you choose, you will also want to bring snacks or even a lunch. For younger children, you should do your research and find destinations that best suit your family's needs. You should also plan when and where to get gas, local lodgings, and food. We've done our best to group these destinations based on nearby towns and cities to help make planning easier.

Dangerous Wildlife

There are several dangerous animals and insects you may encounter while hiking. With a good dose of caution and awareness, you can explore safely. Here are steps you can take to keep yourself and your loved ones safe from dangerous flora and fauna while exploring:

- Keep to the established trails.
- Do not look under rocks, leaves, or sticks.
- Keep hands and feet out of small crawl spaces, bushes, covered areas, or crevices.
- Wear long sleeves and pants to keep arms and legs protected.
- Keep your distance should you encounter any dangerous wildlife or plants.

Limited Cell Service

Do not rely on cell service for navigation or emergencies. Always have a map with you and let someone know where you are and how long you intend to be gone, just in case.

First Aid Information

Always travel with a first aid kit in case of emergencies.

Here are items that you should be certain to include in your primary first aid kit:

- Nitrile gloves
- Blister care products
- Waterproof bandages in multiple sizes
- Ace wrap and athletic tape
- Alcohol wipes and antibiotic ointment
- Irrigation syringe
- Tweezers, nail clippers, trauma shears, safety pins
- Small zip-lock bags for holding contaminated trash

It's a good practice to also keep a secondary first aid kit, especially when hiking, for more serious injuries or medical emergencies. Items in this should include:

- Blood clotting sponges
- Sterile gauze pads
- Trauma pads

- Moist burn pads
- Triangular bandages/sling
- Butterfly strips
- Tincture of benzoin
- Medications (ibuprofen, acetaminophen, antihistamine, aspirin, etc.)
- Thermometer
- CPR mask
- Wilderness medicine handbook
- Antivenin

There is much more to explore, but this is a great start.

For information on all national parks, visit https://www.nps.gov/index.htm.

This site will give you information on up-to-date entrance fees and how to purchase a park pass for unlimited access to national and state parks. This site will also introduce you to all of the trails at each park.

Always check before you travel to destinations to make sure there are no closures. Some hiking trails close when there is heavy rain or snow in the area, and other parks close parts of their land to allow wildlife to migrate. Attractions may change their hours or temporarily shut down for various reasons. Check the websites for the most up-to-date information.